DOVER · THRIFT · EDITIONS

Miss Julie

AUGUST STRINDBERG

DOVER PUBLICATIONS, INC.
New York

DOVER THRIFT EDITIONS
GENERAL EDITOR: STANLEY APPELBAUM
EDITOR OF THIS VOLUME: PHILIP SMITH

Performance

This Dover Thrift Edition may be used in its entirety, in adaptation or in any other way for theatrical productions, professional and amateur, in the United States, without fee, permission or acknowledgment. (This may not apply outside of the United States, as copyright conditions may vary.)

This Dover edition, first published in 1992,
contains an unabridged republication of *Miss Julie*
as originally published as "Miss Julia" in the collection
Plays by August Strindberg, Second Series,
translated with introductions by Edwin Björkman,
Charles Scribner's Sons, New York, 1913.
An introductory Note has been specially prepared
for this edition.

Library of Congress Cataloging-in-Publication Data

Strindberg, August, 1849–1912.
[Fröken Julie. English]
Miss Julie / August Strindberg.
p.   cm. — (Dover thrift editions)
"An unabridged republication of Miss Julie as originally published
in the collection Plays by August Strindberg.
Second series, translated with introductions by Edwin Björkman,
Charles Scribner's Sons, New York, 1913"—T.p. verso.
ISBN-13: 978-0-486-27281-8
ISBN-10: 0-486-27281-8
I. Title.   II. Series.
PT9812.F81E5   1992
839.72'6—dc20   92-15845
CIP

Manufactured in the United States by Courier Corporation
27281809
www.doverpublications.com

Note

THE PRINCIPAL GENIUS of Swedish literature and a pivotal figure in the development of modern drama, August Strindberg (1849–1912) was at the center of the literary controversies that transformed the European stage during the late nineteenth century. During his forty-year career, which helped to establish radical dramatic idioms as diverse as Naturalism and Expressionism, Strindberg gained notoriety both as an insightful portrayer of character and as an unrelenting opponent of the social and theatrical mores and restrictions of his day.

Miss Julie (*Fröken Julie*), the most acclaimed work of Strindberg's Naturalistic period, initially appeared as a printed text in 1888, a year before its first staging. Its nontheatrical debut underscored the play's status as an experimental work—an impression encouraged by the inclusion of a lengthy preface in which the author discussed, with characteristic bluntness, the rationale behind the work's formal innovations and their relation to contemporary artistic norms. In the years since its first publication *Miss Julie* has achieved renown as an unmatched masterpiece of dramatic verisimilitude, and its preface has been hailed as a landmark of literary ideology.

Contents

Author's Preface

LIKE ALMOST ALL other art, that of the stage has long seemed to me a sort of *Biblia Pauperum*, or a Bible in pictures for those who cannot read what is written or printed. And in the same way the playwright has seemed to me a lay preacher spreading the thoughts of his time in a form so popular that the middle classes, from which theatrical audiences are mainly drawn, can know what is being talked about without troubling their brains too much. For this reason the theatre has always served as a grammar-school to young people, women, and those who have acquired a little knowledge, all of whom retain the capacity for deceiving themselves and being deceived—which means again that they are susceptible to illusions produced by the suggestions of the author. And for the same reason I have had a feeling that, in our time, when the rudimentary, incomplete thought processes operating through our fancy seem to be developing into reflection, research, and analysis, the theatre might stand on the verge of being abandoned as a decaying form, for the enjoyment of which we lack the requisite conditions. The prolonged theatrical crisis now prevailing throughout Europe speaks in favour of such a supposition, as well as the fact that, in the civilised countries producing the greatest thinkers of the age, namely, England and Germany, the drama is as dead as are most of the other fine arts.

In some other countries it has, however, been thought possible to create a new drama by filling the old forms with the contents of a new time. But, for one thing, there has not been time for the new thoughts to become so popularised that the public might grasp the questions raised; secondly, minds have been so inflamed by party conflicts that pure and disinterested enjoyment has been excluded from places where one's innermost feelings are violated and the tyranny of an applauding or hissing majority is exercised with the openness for which the theatre gives a chance; and, finally, there has been no new form devised for the new contents, and the new wine has burst the old bottles.

In the following drama I have not tried to do anything new—for that cannot be done—but I have tried to modernise the form in accordance with the demands which I thought the new men of a new time might be likely to make on this art. And with such a purpose in view, I have chosen, or surrendered myself to, a theme that might well be said to lie outside the partisan strife of the day: for the problem of social ascendancy or decline, of higher or lower, of better or worse, of men or women, is, has been, and will be of lasting interest. In selecting this theme from real life, as it was related to me a number of years ago, when the incident impressed me very deeply, I found it suited to a tragedy, because it can only make us sad to see a fortunately placed individual perish, and this must be the case in still higher degree when we see an entire family die out. But perhaps a time will arrive when we have become so developed, so enlightened, that we can remain indifferent before the spectacle of life, which now seems so brutal, so cynical, so heartless; when we have closed up those lower, unreliable instruments of thought which we call feelings, and which have been rendered not only superfluous but harmful by the final growth of our reflective organs.

The fact that the heroine arouses our pity depends only on our weakness in not being able to resist the sense of fear that the same fate could befall ourselves. And yet it is possible that a very sensitive spectator might fail to find satisfaction in this kind of pity, while the man believing in the future might demand some positive suggestion for the abolition of evil, or, in other words, some kind of programme. But, first of all, there is no absolute evil. That one family perishes is the fortune of another family, which thereby gets a chance to rise. And the alternation of ascent and descent constitutes one of life's main charms, as fortune is solely determined by comparison. And to the man with a programme, who wants to remedy the sad circumstance that the hawk eats the dove, and the flea eats the hawk, I have this question to put: why should it be remedied? Life is not so mathematically idiotic that it lets only the big eat the small, but it happens just as often that the bee kills the lion, or drives it to madness at least.

That my tragedy makes a sad impression on many is their own fault. When we grow strong as were the men of the first French revolution, then we shall receive an unconditionally good and joyful impression from seeing the national forests rid of rotting and superannuated trees that have stood too long in the way of others with equal right to a period of free growth—an impression good in the same way as that received from the death of one incurably diseased.

Not long ago they reproached my tragedy "The Father" with being too sad—just as if they wanted merry tragedies. Everybody is clamouring arrogantly for "the joy of life," and all theatrical managers are giving orders for farces, as if the joy of life consisted in being silly and picturing all human beings as so many sufferers from St. Vitus' dance or idiocy. I find the joy of life in its violent and cruel struggles, and my pleasure lies in knowing something and learning something. And for this reason I have selected an unusual but instructive case—an exception, in a word—but a great exception, proving the rule, which, of course, will provoke all lovers of the commonplace. And what also will offend simple brains is that my action cannot be traced back to a single motive, that the viewpoint is not always the same. An event in real life—and this discovery is quite recent—springs generally from a whole series of more or less deeplying motives, but of these the spectator chooses as a rule the one his reason can master most easily, or else the one reflecting most favourably on his power of reasoning. A suicide is committed. Bad business, says the merchant. Unrequited love, say the ladies. Sickness, says the sick man. Crushed hopes, says the shipwrecked. But now it may be that the motive lay in all or none of these directions. It is possible that the one who is dead may have hid the main motive by pushing forward another meant to place his memory in a better light.

In explanation of *Miss Julie's* sad fate I have suggested many factors: her mother's fundamental instincts; her father's mistaken upbringing of the girl; her own nature, and the suggestive influence of her fiancé on a weak and degenerate brain; furthermore, and more directly: the festive mood of the Midsummer Eve; the absence of her father; her physical condition; her preoccupation with the animals; the excitation of the dance; the dusk of the night; the strongly aphrodisiacal influence of the flowers; and lastly the chance forcing the two of them together in a secluded room, to which must be added the aggressiveness of the excited man.

Thus I have neither been one-sidedly physiological nor one-sidedly psychological in my procedure. Nor have I merely delivered a moral preachment. This multiplicity of motives I regard as praiseworthy because it is in keeping with the views of our own time. And if others have done the same thing before me, I may boast of not being the sole inventor of my paradoxes—as all discoveries are named.

In regard to the character-drawing I may say that I have tried to make my figures rather "characterless," and I have done so for reasons I shall now state.

In the course of the ages the word character has assumed many meanings. Originally it signified probably the dominant groundnote in the complex mass of the self, and as such it was confused with temperament. Afterward it became the middle-class term for an automaton, so that an individual whose nature had come to a stand-still, or who had adapted himself to a certain part in life—who had ceased to grow, in a word—was named a character; while one remaining in a state of development—a skilful navigator on life's river, who did not sail with close-tied sheets, but knew when to fall off before the wind and when to luff again—was called lacking in character. And he was called so in a depreciatory sense, of course, because he was so hard to catch, to classify, and to keep track of. This middle-class notion about the immobility of the soul was transplanted to the stage, where the middle-class element has always held sway. There a character became synonymous with a gentleman fixed and finished once for all—one who invariably appeared drunk, jolly, sad. And for the purpose of characterisation nothing more was needed than some physical deformity like a club-foot, a wooden leg, a red nose; or the person concerned was made to repeat some phrase like "That's capital!" or "Barkis is willin'," or something of that kind. This manner of regarding human beings as homogeneous is preserved even by the great Molière. *Harpagon* is nothing but miserly, although *Harpagon* might as well have been at once miserly and a financial genius, a fine father, and a public-spirited citizen. What is worse yet, his "defect" is of distinct advantage to his son-in-law and daughter, who are his heirs, and for that reason should not find fault with him, even if they have to wait a little for their wedding. I do not believe, therefore, in simple characters on the stage. And the summary judgments of the author upon men—this one stupid, and that one brutal, this one jealous, and that one stingy— should be challenged by the naturalists, who know the fertility of the soul-complex, and who realise that "vice" has a reverse very much resembling virtue.

Because they are modern characters, living in a period of transition more hysterically hurried than its immediate predecessor at least, I have made my figures vacillating, out of joint, torn between the old and the new. And I do not think it unlikely that, through newspaper reading and overheard conversations, modern ideas may have leaked down to the strata where domestic servants belong.

My souls (or characters) are conglomerates, made up of past and present stages of civilisation, scraps of humanity, torn-off pieces of Sunday clothing turned into rags—all patched together as is the human soul itself. And I have furthermore offered a touch of evolutionary history by letting the weaker repeat words stolen from the stronger, and by letting different souls accept "ideas"—or suggestions, as they are called—from each other.

Miss Julie is a modern character, not because the man-hating half-woman may not have existed in all ages, but because now, after her discovery, she has stepped to the front and begun to make a noise. The half-woman is a type coming more and more into prominence, selling herself nowadays for power, decorations, distinctions, diplomas, as formerly for money, and the type indicates degeneration. It is not a good type, for it does not last, but unfortunately it has the power of reproducing itself and its misery through one more generation. And degenerate men seem instinctively to make their selection from this kind of women, so that they multiply and produce indeterminate sexes to whom life is a torture. Fortunately, however, they perish in the end, either from discord with real life, or from the irresistible revolt of their suppressed instincts, or from foiled hopes of possessing the man. The type is tragical, offering us the spectacle of a desperate struggle against nature. It is also tragical as a Romantic inheritance dispersed by the prevailing Naturalism, which wants nothing but happiness: and for happiness strong and sound races are required.

But *Miss Julie* is also a remnant of the old military nobility which is now giving way to the new nobility of nerves and brain. She is a victim of the discord which a mother's "crime" produces in a family, and also a victim of the day's delusions, of the circumstances, of her defective constitution—all of which may be held equivalent to the old-fashioned fate or universal law. The naturalist has wiped out the idea of guilt, but he cannot wipe out the results of an action—punishment, prison, or fear—and for the simple reason that they remain without regard to his verdict. For fellow-beings that have been wronged are not so good-natured as those on the outside, who have not been wronged at all, can be without cost to themselves.

Even if, for reasons over which he could have no control, the father should forego his vengeance, the daughter would take vengeance upon herself, just as she does in the play, and she would be moved to it by that innate or acquired sense of honour which the upper classes inherit—whence? From the days of barbarism, from the original home of the Aryans, from the chivalry of the Middle Ages? It is beautiful, but it has become disadvantageous to the preservation of the race. It is this, the nobleman's *harakiri*—or the law of the inner conscience compelling the Japanese to cut open his own abdomen at the insult of another—which survives, though somewhat modified, in the duel, also a privilege of the nobility. For this reason the valet, *Jean*, continues to live, but *Miss Julie* cannot live on without honour. In so far as he lacks this life-endangering superstition about honour, the serf takes precedence of the earl, and in all of us Aryans there is something of the nobleman, or of Don Quixote, which makes us sympathise with the man who takes his own life because he has committed a dishonourable deed and thus lost his honour. And we are noblemen to the extent of suffering from seeing the earth littered with the living corpse of one who was once great—yes, even if the one thus fallen should rise again and make restitution by honourable deeds.

Jean, the valet, is of the kind that builds new stock—one in whom the differentiation is clearly noticeable. He was a cotter's child, and he has trained himself up to the point where the future gentleman has become visible. He has found it easy to learn, having finely developed senses (smell, taste, vision) and an instinct for beauty besides. He has already risen in the world, and is strong enough not to be sensitive about using other people's services. He has already become a stranger to his equals, despising them as so many outlived stages, but also fearing and fleeing them because they know his secrets, pry into his plans, watch his rise with envy, and look forward to his fall with pleasure. From this relationship springs his dual, indeterminate character, oscillating between love of distinction and hatred of those who have already achieved it. He says himself that he is an aristocrat, and has learned the secrets of good company. He is polished on the outside and coarse within. He knows already how to wear the frock-coat with ease, but the cleanliness of his body cannot be guaranteed.

He feels respect for the young lady, but he is afraid of *Christine*, who has his dangerous secrets in her keeping. His emotional callousness is sufficient to prevent the night's happenings from exercising a disturbing influence on his plans for the future. Having at once the slave's brutality and the master's lack of squeamishness, he can see blood without fainting, and he can also bend his back under a mishap until able to throw it off. For this reason he will emerge unharmed from the battle, and will probably end his days as the owner of a hotel. And if he does not become a Roumanian count, his son will probably go to a university, and may even become a county attorney.

Otherwise, he furnishes us with rather significant information as to the way in which the lower classes look at life from beneath—that is, when he speaks the truth, which is not often, as he prefers what seems favourable to himself to what is true. When *Miss Julie* suggests that the lower classes must feel the pressure from above very heavily, *Jean* agrees with her, of course, because he wants to gain her sympathy. But he corrects himself at once, the moment he realises the advantage of standing apart from the herd.

And *Jean* stands above *Miss Julie* not only because his fate is in ascendancy, but because he is a man. Sexually he is the aristocrat because of his male strength, his more finely developed senses, and his capacity for taking the initiative. His inferiority depends mainly on the temporary social environment in which he has to live, and which he probably can shed together with the valet's livery.

The mind of the slave speaks through his reverence for the count (as shown in the incident with the boots) and through his religious superstition. But he reveres the count principally as a possessor of that higher position toward which he himself is striving. And this reverence remains even when he has won the daughter of the house, and seen that the beautiful shell covered nothing but emptiness.

I don't believe that any love relation in a "higher" sense can spring up between two souls of such different quality. And for this reason I let *Miss Julie* imagine her love to be protective or commiserative in its origin. And I let *Jean* suppose that, under different social conditions, he might feel something like real love for her. I believe love to be like the hyacinth, which has to strike roots in darkness *before* it can bring forth a vigorous flower. In this case it shoots up quickly, bringing forth blossom and seed at once, and for that reason the plant withers so soon.

Christine, finally, is a female slave, full of servility and sluggishness acquired in front of the kitchen fire, and stuffed full of morality and religion that are meant to serve her at once as cloak and scapegoat. Her church-going has for its purpose to bring her quick and easy riddance of all responsibility for her domestic thieveries and to equip her with a new stock of guiltlessness. Otherwise she is a subordinate figure, and therefore purposely sketched in the same manner as the minister and the doctor in "The Father," whom I designed as ordinary human beings, like the common run of country ministers and country doctors. And if these accessory characters have seemed mere abstractions to some people, it depends on the fact that ordinary men are to a certain extent impersonal in the exercise of their callings. This means that they are without individuality, showing only one side of themselves while at work. And as long as the spectator does not feel the need of seeing them from other sides, my abstract presentation of them remains on the whole correct.

In regard to the dialogue, I want to point out that I have departed somewhat from prevailing traditions by not turning my figures into catechists who make stupid questions in order to call forth witty answers. I have avoided the symmetrical and mathematical construction of the

French dialogue, and have instead permitted the minds to work irregularly as they do in reality, where, during conversation, the cogs of one mind seem more or less haphazardly to engage those of another one, and where no topic is fully exhausted. Naturally enough, therefore, the dialogue strays a good deal as, in the opening scenes, it acquires a material that later on is worked over, picked up again, repeated, expounded, and built up like the theme in a musical composition.

The plot is pregnant enough, and as, at bottom, it is concerned only with two persons, I have concentrated my attention on these, introducing only one subordinate figure, the cook, and keeping the unfortunate spirit of the father hovering above and beyond the action. I have done this because I believe I have noticed that the psychological processes are what interest the people of our own day more than anything else. Our souls, so eager for knowledge, cannot rest satisfied with seeing what happens, but must also learn how it comes to happen! What we want to see are just the wires, the machinery. We want to investigate the box with the false bottom, touch the magic ring in order to find the suture, and look into the cards to discover how they are marked.

In this I have taken for models the monographic novels of the brothers de Goncourt, which have appealed more to me than any other modern literature.

Turning to the technical side of the composition, I have tried to abolish the division into acts. And I have done so because I have come to fear that our decreasing capacity for illusion might be unfavourably affected by intermissions during which the spectator would have time to reflect and to get away from the suggestive influence of the author-hypnotist. My play will probably last an hour and a half, and as it is possible to listen that length of time, or longer, to a lecture, a sermon, or a debate, I have imagined that a theatrical performance could not become fatiguing in the same time. As early as 1872, in one of my first dramatic experiments, "The Outlaw," I tried the same concentrated form, but with scant success. The play was written in five acts and wholly completed when I became aware of the restless, scattered effect it produced. Then I burned it, and out of the ashes rose a single, well-built act, covering fifty printed pages, and taking an hour for its performance. Thus the form of the present play is not new, but it seems to be my own, and changing æsthetical conventions may possibly make it timely.

My hope is still for a public educated to the point where it can sit through a whole-evening performance in a single act. But that point cannot be reached without a great deal of experimentation. In the meantime I have resorted to three art forms that are to provide resting-places for the public and the actors, without letting the public escape from the illusion induced. All these forms are subsidiary to the drama. They are the monologue, the pantomime, and the dance, all of them belonging originally to the tragedy of classical antiquity. For the monologue has sprung from the monody, and the chorus has developed into the ballet.

Our realists have excommunicated the monologue as improbable, but if I can lay a proper basis for it, I can also make it seem probable, and then I can use it to good advantage. It is probable, for instance, that a speaker may walk back and forth in his room practising his speech aloud; it is probable that an actor may read through his part aloud, that a servant-girl may talk to her cat, that a mother may prattle to her child, that an old spinster may chatter to her parrot, that a person may talk in his sleep. And in order that the actor for once may have a chance to work independently, and to be free for a moment from the author's pointer, it is better that the monologues be not written out, but just indicated. As it matters comparatively little what is said to the parrot or the cat, or in one's sleep—because it cannot influence the action—it is possible that a gifted actor, carried away by the situation and the mood of the occasion, may improvise such matters better than they could be written by the author, who cannot figure out in advance how much may be said, and how long the talk may last, without waking the public out of their illusions.

It is well known that, on certain stages, the Italian theatre has returned to improvisation and thereby produced creative actors—who, however, must follow the author's suggestions—and this may be counted a step forward, or even the beginning of a new art form that might well be called *productive*.

Where, on the other hand, the monologue would seem unreal, I have used the pantomime, and there I have left still greater scope for the actor's imagination—and for his desire to gain independent honours. But in order that the public may not be tried beyond endurance, I have permitted the music—which is amply warranted by the Midsummer Eve's dance—to exercise its illusory power while the dumb show lasts. And I ask the musical director to make careful selection of the music used for this purpose, so that incompatible moods are not induced by reminiscences from the last musical comedy or topical song, or by folk-tunes of too markedly ethnographical distinction.

The mere introduction of a scene with a lot of "people" could not have taken the place of the dance, for such scenes are poorly acted and tempt a number of grinning idiots into displaying their own smartness, whereby the illusion is disturbed. As the common people do not improvise their gibes, but use ready-made phrases in which stick some double meaning, I have not composed their lampooning song, but have appropriated a little known folk-dance which I personally noted down in a district near Stockholm. The words don't quite hit the point, but hint vaguely at it, and this is intentional, for the cunning (*i.e.*, weakness) of the slave keeps him from any direct attack. There must, then, be no chattering clowns in a serious action, and no coarse flouting at a situation that puts the lid on the coffin of a whole family.

As far as the scenery is concerned, I have borrowed from impressionistic painting its asymmetry, its quality of abruptness, and have thereby in my opinion strengthened the illusion. Because the whole room and all its contents are not shown, there is a chance to guess at things—that is, our imagination is stirred into complementing our vision. I have made a further gain in getting rid of those tiresome exits by means of doors, especially as stage doors are made of canvas and swing back and forth at the lightest touch. They are not even capable of expressing the anger of an irate *pater familias* who, on leaving his home after a poor dinner, slams the door behind him "so that it shakes the whole house." (On the stage the house sways.) I have also contented myself with a single setting, and for the double purpose of making the figures become parts of their surroundings, and of breaking with the tendency toward luxurious scenery. But having only a single setting, one may demand to have it real. Yet nothing is more difficult than to get a room that looks something like a room, although the painter can easily enough produce waterfalls and flaming volcanoes. Let it go at canvas for the walls, but we might be done with the painting of shelves and kitchen utensils on the canvas. We have so much else on the stage that is conventional, and in which we are asked to believe, that we might at least be spared the too great effort of believing in painted pans and kettles.

I have placed the rear wall and the table diagonally across the stage in order to make the actors show full face and half profile to the audience when they sit opposite each other at the table. In the opera "Aïda" I noticed an oblique background, which led the eye out into unseen prospects. And it did not appear to be the result of any reaction against the fatiguing right angle.

Another novelty well needed would be the abolition of the foot-lights. The light from below is said to have for its purpose to make the faces of the actors look fatter. But I cannot help asking: why must all actors be fat in the face? Does not this light from below tend to wipe out the subtler lineaments in the lower part of the face, and especially around the jaws? Does it not give a false appearance to the nose and cast shadows upward over the eyes? If this be not so, another thing is certain: namely, that the eyes of the actors suffer from the light, so that the effective play of their glances is precluded. Coming from below, the light strikes the retina in places generally protected (except in sailors, who have to see the sun reflected in the water), and for this reason one observes hardly anything but a vulgar rolling of the eyes, either sideways or upwards, toward the galleries, so that nothing but the white of the eye shows. Perhaps the same cause may account for the tedious blinking of which especially the actresses are guilty. And when anybody on the stage wants to use his eyes to speak with, no other way is left him but the poor one of staring straight at the public, with whom he or she then gets into direct communication outside of the frame provided by the setting. This vicious habit has, rightly or wrongly, been named "to meet friends." Would it not be possible by means of strong side-lights (obtained by the employment of reflectors, for instance) to add to the resources already possessed by the actor? Could not his mimicry be still further strengthened by use of the greatest asset possessed by the face: the play of the eyes?

Of course, I have no illusions about getting the actors to play *for* the public and not *at* it, although such a change would be highly desirable. I dare not even dream of beholding the actor's back throughout an important scene, but I wish with all my heart that crucial scenes might not be played in the centre of the proscenium, like duets meant to bring forth applause. Instead, I should like to have them laid in the place indicated by the situation. Thus I ask for no revolutions, but only for a few minor modifications. To make a real room of the stage, with the fourth wall missing, and a part of the furniture placed back toward the audience, would probably produce a disturbing effect at present.

In wishing to speak of the facial make-up, I have no hope that the ladies will listen to me, as they would rather look beautiful than lifelike. But the actor might consider whether it be to his advantage to paint his face so that it shows some abstract type which covers it like a mask. Suppose that a man puts a markedly choleric line between the eyes, and imagine further that some remark demands a smile of this face fixed in a state of continuous wrath. What a horrible grimace will be the result? And how can the wrathful old man produce a frown on his false forehead, which is smooth as a billiard ball?

In modern psychological dramas, where the subtlest movements of the soul are to be reflected on the face rather than by gestures and noise, it would probably be well to experiment with strong side-light on a small stage, and with unpainted faces, or at least with a minimum of make-up.

If, in addition, we might escape the visible orchestra, with its disturbing lamps and its faces turned toward the public; if we could have the seats on the main floor (the orchestra or the pit) raised so that the eyes of the spectators would be above the knees of the actors; if we could get rid of the boxes with their tittering parties of diners; if we could also have the auditorium completely darkened during the performance; and if, first and last, we could have a small stage and a small house: then a new dramatic art might rise, and the theatre might at least become an institution for the entertainment of people with culture. While waiting for this kind of theatre, I suppose we shall have to write for the "ice-box," and thus prepare the repertory that is to come.

I have made an attempt. If it prove a failure, there is plenty of time to try over again.

Dramatis Personæ

MISS JULIE, *aged twenty-five*

JEAN, *a valet, aged thirty*

CHRISTINE, *a cook, aged thirty-five*

The action takes place on Midsummer Eve, in the kitchen of the Count's country house.

Miss Julie

A Naturalistic Tragedy

1888

Miss Julie

SCENE

A large kitchen: the ceiling and the side walls are hidden by draperies and hangings. The rear wall runs diagonally across the stage, from the left side and away from the spectators. On this wall, to the left, there are two shelves full of utensils made of copper, iron, and tin. The shelves are trimmed with scalloped paper.

A little to the right may be seen three-fourths of the big arched doorway leading to the outside. It has double glass doors, through which are seen a fountain with a cupid, lilac shrubs in bloom, and the tops of some Lombardy poplars.

On the left side of the stage is seen the corner of a big cook-stove built of glazed bricks; also a part of the smoke-hood above it.

From the right protrudes one end of the servants' dining-table of white pine, with a few chairs about it.

The stove is dressed with bundled branches of birch. Twigs of juniper are scattered on the floor.

On the table end stands a big Japanese spice pot full of lilac blossoms.

An icebox, a kitchen-table, and a wash-stand.

Above the door hangs a big old-fashioned bell on a steel spring, and the mouthpiece of a speaking-tube appears at the left of the door.

CHRISTINE *is standing by the stove, frying something in a pan. She has on a dress of light-coloured cotton, which she has covered up with a big kitchen apron.*

JEAN *enters, dressed in livery and carrying a pair of big, spurred riding-boots, which he places on the floor in such a manner that they remain visible to the spectators.*

1

JEAN. To-night Miss Julie is crazy again; absolutely crazy.

CHRISTINE. So you're back again?

JEAN. I took the count to the station, and when I came back by the barn, I went in and had a dance, and there I saw the young lady leading the dance with the gamekeeper. But when she caught sight of me, she rushed right up to me and asked me to dance the ladies' waltz with her. And ever since she's been waltzing like—well, I never saw the like of it. She's crazy!

CHRISTINE. And has always been, but never the way it's been this last fortnight, since her engagement was broken.

JEAN. Well, what kind of a story was that anyhow? He's a fine fellow, isn't he, although he isn't rich? Ugh, but they're so full of notions. [*Sits down at the end of the table*] It's peculiar anyhow, that a young lady—hm!—would rather stay at home with the servants—don't you think?—than go with her father to their relatives!

CHRISTINE. Oh, I guess she feels sort of embarrassed by that rumpus with her fellow.

JEAN. Quite likely. But there was some backbone to that man just the same. Do you know how it happened, Christine? I saw it, although I didn't care to let on.

CHRISTINE. No, did you?

JEAN. Sure, I did. They were in the stable-yard one evening, and the young lady was training him, as she called it. Do you know what that meant? She made him leap over her horse-whip the way you teach a dog to jump. Twice he jumped and got a cut each time. The third time he took the whip out of her hand and broke it into a thousand bits. And then he got out.

CHRISTINE. So that's the way it happened! You don't say!

JEAN. Yes, that's how that thing happened. Well, Christine, what have you got that's tasty?

CHRISTINE. [*Serves from the pan and puts the plate before Jean*] Oh, just some kidney which I cut out of the veal roast.

JEAN. [*Smelling the food*] Fine! That's my great *délice*. [*Feeling the plate*] But you might have warmed the plate.

CHRISTINE. Well, if you ain't harder to please than the count himself!
[*Pulls his hair playfully.*

JEAN. [*Irritated*] Don't pull my hair! You know how sensitive I am.

CHRISTINE. Well, well, it was nothing but a love pull, you know.

JEAN *eats.*
CHRISTINE *opens a bottle of beer.*

JEAN. Beer—on Midsummer Eve? No, thank you! Then I have something better myself. [*Opens a table-drawer and takes out a bottle of claret with yellow cap*] Yellow seal, mind you! Give me a glass—and you use those with stems when you drink it *pure*.

CHRISTINE. [*Returns to the stove and puts a small pan on the fire*] Heaven preserve her that gets you for a husband, Mr. Finicky!

JEAN. Oh, rot! You'd be glad enough to get a smart fellow like me. And I guess it hasn't hurt you that they call me your beau. [*Tasting the wine*] Good! Pretty good! Just a tiny bit too cold. [*He warms the glass with his hands*] We got this at Dijon. It cost us four francs per litre, not counting the bottle. And there was the duty besides. What is it you're cooking—with that infernal smell?

CHRISTINE. Oh, it's some deviltry the young lady is going to give Diana.

JEAN. You should choose your words with more care, Christine. But why should you be cooking for a bitch on a holiday eve like this? Is she sick?

CHRISTINE. Ye-es, she is sick. She's been running around with the gate-keeper's pug—and now there's trouble—and the young lady just won't hear of it.

JEAN. The young lady is too stuck up in some ways and not proud enough in others—just as was the countess while she lived. She was most at home in the kitchen and among the cows, but she would never drive with only one horse. She wore her cuffs till they were dirty, but she had to have cuff buttons with a coronet on them. And speaking of the young lady, she doesn't take proper care of herself and her person. I might even say that she's lacking in refinement. Just now, when she was dancing in the barn, she pulled the gamekeeper away from Anna and asked him herself to come and dance with her. We wouldn't act in that way. But that's just how it is: when upper-class people want to demean themselves, then they grow—mean! But she's splendid! Magnificent! Oh, such shoulders! And—and so on!

CHRISTINE. Oh, well, don't brag too much! I've heard Clara talking, who tends to her dressing.

JEAN. Pooh, Clara! You're always jealous of each other. I, who have been out riding with her— And then the way she dances!

CHRISTINE. Say, Jean, won't you dance with me when I'm done?

JEAN. Of course I will.

CHRISTINE. Do you promise?

JEAN. Promise? When I say so, I'll do it. Well, here's thanks for the good food. It tasted fine!   [*Puts the cork back into the bottle.*

JULIE. [*Appears in the doorway, speaking to somebody on the outside*] I'll be back in a minute. You go right on in the meantime.

JEAN *slips the bottle into the table-drawer and rises respectfully.*

JULIE. [*Enters and goes over to* CHRISTINE *by the wash-stand*] Well, is it done yet?

CHRISTINE *signs to her that* JEAN *is present.*

JEAN. [*Gallantly*] The ladies are having secrets, I believe.

JULIE. [*Strikes him in the face with her handkerchief*] That's for you, Mr. Pry!

JEAN. Oh, what a delicious odor that violet has!

JULIE. [*With coquetry*] Impudent! So you know something about perfumes also? And know pretty well how to dance— Now don't peep! Go away!

JEAN. [*With polite impudence*] Is it some kind of witches' broth the ladies are cooking on Midsummer Eve—something to tell fortunes by and bring out the lucky star in which one's future love is seen?

JULIE. [*Sharply*] If you can see that, you'll have good eyes, indeed! [*To* CHRISTINE] Put it in a pint bottle and cork it well. Come and dance a *schottische* with me now, Jean.

JEAN. [*Hesitatingly*] I don't want to be impolite, but I had promised to dance with Christine this time——

JULIE. Well, she can get somebody else—can't you, Christine? Won't you let me borrow Jean from you?

CHRISTINE. That isn't for me to say. When Miss Julie is so gracious, it isn't for him to say no. You just go along, and be thankful for the honour, too!

JEAN. Frankly speaking, but not wishing to offend in any way, I cannot help wondering if it's wise for Miss Julie to dance twice in succession with the same partner, especially as the people here are not slow in throwing out hints——

JULIE. [*Flaring up*] What is that? What kind of hints? What do you mean?

JEAN. [*Submissively*] As you don't want to understand, I have to speak more plainly. It don't look well to prefer one servant to all the rest who are expecting to be honoured in the same unusual way——

JULIE. Prefer! What ideas! I'm surprised! I, the mistress of the house, deign to honour this dance with my presence, and when it so happens that I actually want to dance, I want to dance with one who knows how to lead, so that I am not made ridiculous.

JEAN. As you command, Miss Julie! I am at your service!

JULIE. [*Softened*] Don't take it as a command. To-night we should enjoy ourselves as a lot of happy people, and all rank should be forgotten. Now give me your arm. Don't be afraid, Christine! I'll return your beau to you!

JEAN *offers his arm to* MISS JULIE *and leads her out.*

PANTOMIME

Must be acted as if the actress were really alone in the place. When necessary she turns her back to the public. She should not look in the direction of the spectators, and she should not hurry as if fearful that they might become impatient.
CHRISTINE *is alone. A schottische tune played on a violin is heard faintly in the distance.*
While humming the tune, CHRISTINE *clears off the table after* JEAN, *washes the plate at the kitchen table, wipes it, and puts it away in a cupboard.*
Then she takes off her apron, pulls out a small mirror from one of the table-drawers and leans it against the flower jar on the table; lights a tallow candle and heats a hairpin, which she uses to curl her front hair.
Then she goes to the door and stands there listening. Returns to the table. Discovers the handkerchief which MISS JULIE *has left behind, picks it up, and smells it, spreads it out absent-mindedly and begins to stretch it, smooth it, fold it up, and so forth.*

JEAN. [*Enters alone*] Crazy, that's what she is! The way she dances! And the people stand behind the doors and grin at her. What do you think of it, Christine?

CHRISTINE. Oh, she has her time now, and then she is always a little queer like that. But are you going to dance with me now?

JEAN. You are not mad at me because I disappointed you?

CHRISTINE. No!—Not for a little thing like that, you know! And also, I know my place——

JEAN. [*Putting his arm around her waist*] You are a sensible girl, Christine, and I think you'll make a good wife——

JULIE. [*Enters and is unpleasantly surprised; speaks with forced gayety*] Yes, you are a fine partner—running away from your lady!

JEAN. On the contrary, Miss Julie. I have, as you see, looked up the one I deserted.

JULIE. [*Changing tone*] Do you know, there is nobody that dances like you!—But why do you wear your livery on an evening like this? Take it off at once!

JEAN. Then I must ask you to step outside for a moment, as my black coat is hanging right here.

> [*Points toward the right and goes in that direction.*

JULIE. Are you bashful on my account? Just to change a coat? Why don't you go into your own room and come back again? Or, you can stay right here, and I'll turn my back on you.

JEAN. With your permission, Miss Julie.

> *Goes further over to the right; one of his arms can be seen as he changes his coat.*

JULIE. [*To* CHRISTINE] Are you and Jean engaged, that he's so familiar with you?

CHRISTINE. Engaged? Well, in a way. We call it that.

JULIE. Call it?

CHRISTINE. Well, Miss Julie, you have had a fellow of your own, and——

JULIE. We were really engaged——

CHRISTINE. But it didn't come to anything just the same——

> JEAN *enters, dressed in black frock-coat and black derby.*

JULIE. *Très gentil, Monsieur Jean! Très gentil!*

JEAN. *Vous voulez plaisanter, Madame!*

JULIE. *Et vous voulez parler français!* Where did you learn it?

JEAN. In Switzerland, while I worked as *sommelier* in one of the big hotels at Lucerne.

JULIE. But you look like a real gentleman in your frock-coat! Charming!

> [*Sits down at the table.*

JEAN. Oh, you flatter me.

JULIE. [*Offended*] Flatter—you!

JEAN. My natural modesty does not allow me to believe that you could be paying genuine compliments to one like me, and so I dare to assume that you are exaggerating, or, as we call it, flattering.

JULIE. Where did you learn to use your words like that? You must have been to the theatre a great deal?

JEAN. That, too. I have been to a lot of places.

JULIE. But you were born in this neighbourhood?

JEAN. My father was a cotter on the county attorney's property right by here, and I can recall seeing you as a child, although you, of course, didn't notice me.

JULIE. No, really!

JEAN. Yes, and I remember one time in particular—but of that I can't speak.

JULIE. Oh, yes, do! Why—just for once.

JEAN. No, really, I cannot do it now. Another time, perhaps.

JULIE. Another time is no time. Is it as bad as that?

JEAN. It isn't bad, but it comes a little hard. Look at that one!

Points to CHRISTINE, *who has fallen asleep on a chair by the stove.*

JULIE. She'll make a pleasant wife. And perhaps she snores, too.

JEAN. No, she doesn't, but she talks in her sleep.

JULIE. [*Cynically*] How do you know?

JEAN. [*Insolently*] I have heard it.

Pause during which they study each other.

JULIE. Why don't you sit down?

JEAN. It wouldn't be proper in your presence.

JULIE. But if I order you to do it?

JEAN. Then I obey.

JULIE. Sit down, then!—But wait a moment! Can you give me something to drink first?

JEAN. I don't know what we have got in the icebox. I fear it is nothing but beer.

JULIE. And you call that nothing? My taste is so simple that I prefer it to wine.

JEAN. [*Takes a bottle of beer from the icebox and opens it; gets a glass and a plate from the cupboard, and serves the beer*] Allow me!

JULIE. Thank you. Don't you want some yourself?

JEAN. I don't care very much for beer, but if it is a command, of course——

JULIE. Command?—I should think a polite gentleman might keep his lady company.

JEAN. Yes, that's the way it should be.

[*Opens another bottle and takes out a glass.*]

JULIE. Drink my health now!

JEAN *hesitates.*

JULIE. Are you bashful—a big, grown-up man?

JEAN. [*Kneels with mock solemnity and raises his glass*] To the health of my liege lady!

JULIE. Bravo!—And now you must also kiss my shoe in order to get it just right.

> JEAN *hesitates a moment; then he takes hold of her foot and touches it lightly with his lips.*

JULIE. Excellent! You should have been on the stage.

JEAN. [*Rising to his feet*] This won't do any longer, Miss Julie. Somebody might see us.

JULIE. What would that matter?

JEAN. Oh, it would set the people talking—that's all! And if you only knew how their tongues were wagging up there a while ago——

JULIE. What did they have to say? Tell me— Sit down now!

JEAN. [*Sits down*] I don't want to hurt you, but they were using expressions—which cast reflections of a kind that—oh, you know it yourself! You are not a child, and when a lady is seen alone with a man, drinking—no matter if he's only a servant—and at night—then——

JULIE. Then what? And besides, we are not alone. Isn't Christine with us?

JEAN. Yes—asleep!

JULIE. Then I'll wake her. [*Rising*] Christine, are you asleep?

CHRISTINE. [*In her sleep*] Blub-blub-blub-blub!

JULIE. Christine!—Did you ever see such a sleeper.

CHRISTINE. [*In her sleep*] The count's boots are polished—put on the coffee—yes, yes, yes—my-my—pooh!

JULIE. [*Pinches her nose*] Can't you wake up?

JEAN. [*Sternly*] You shouldn't bother those that sleep.

JULIE. [*Sharply*] What's that?

JEAN. One who has stood by the stove all day has a right to be tired at night. And sleep should be respected.

JULIE. [*Changing tone*] It is fine to think like that, and it does you honour—I thank you for it. [*Gives* JEAN *her hand*] Come now and pick some lilacs for me.

> *During the following scene* CHRISTINE *wakes up. She moves as if still asleep and goes out to the right in order to go to bed.*

JEAN. With you, Miss Julie?

JULIE. With me!

JEAN. But it won't do! Absolutely not!

JULIE. I can't understand what you are thinking of. You couldn't possibly imagine——

JEAN. No, not I, but the people.

JULIE. What? That I am fond of the valet?

JEAN. I am not at all conceited, but such things have happened—and to the people nothing is sacred.

JULIE. You are an aristocrat, I think.

JEAN. Yes, I am.

JULIE. And I am stepping down——

JEAN. Take my advice, Miss Julie, don't step down. Nobody will believe you did it on purpose. The people will always say that you fell down.

JULIE. I think better of the people than you do. Come and see if I am not right. Come along!   [*She ogles him.*

JEAN. You're mighty queer, do you know!

JULIE. Perhaps. But so are you. And for that matter, everything is queer. Life, men, everything—just a mush that floats on top of the water until it sinks, sinks down! I have a dream that comes back to me ever so often. And just now I am reminded of it. I have climbed to the top of a column and sit there without being able to tell how to get down again. I get dizzy when I look down, and I must get down, but I haven't the courage to jump off. I cannot hold on, and I am longing to fall, and yet I don't fall. But there will be no rest for me until I get down, no rest until I get down, down on the ground. And if I did reach the ground, I should want to get still further down, into the ground itself— Have you ever felt like that?

JEAN. No, my dream is that I am lying under a tall tree in a dark wood. I want to get up, up to the top, so that I can look out over the smiling landscape, where the sun is shining, and so that I can rob the nest in which lie the golden eggs. And I climb and climb, but the trunk is so thick and smooth, and it is so far to the first branch. But I know that if I could only reach that first branch, then I should go right on to the top as on a ladder. I have not reached it yet, but I am going to, if it only be in my dreams.

JULIE. Here I am chattering to you about dreams! Come along! Only into the park!

She offers her arm to him, and they go toward the door.

JEAN. We must sleep on nine midsummer flowers to-night, Miss Julie—then our dreams will come true.

They turn around in the doorway, and JEAN *puts one hand up to his eyes.*

JULIE. Let me see what you have got in your eye.

JEAN. Oh, nothing—just some dirt—it will soon be gone.

JULIE. It was my sleeve that rubbed against it. Sit down and let me help you. [*Takes him by the arm and makes him sit down; takes hold of his head and bends it backwards; tries to get out the dirt with a corner of her handkerchief*] Sit still now, absolutely still! [*Slaps him on the hand*] Well, can't you do as I say? I think you are shaking—a big, strong fellow like you! [*Feels his biceps*] And with such arms!

JEAN. [*Ominously*] Miss Julie!

JULIE. Yes, Monsieur Jean.

JEAN. *Attention! Je ne suis qu'un homme.*

JULIE. Can't you sit still!— There now! Now it's gone. Kiss my hand now, and thank me.

JEAN. [*Rising*] Miss Julie, listen to me. Christine has gone to bed now— Won't you listen to me?

JULIE. Kiss my hand first.

JEAN. Listen to me!

JULIE. Kiss my hand first!

JEAN. All right, but blame nobody but yourself!

JULIE. For what?

JEAN. For what? Are you still a mere child at twenty-five? Don't you know that it is dangerous to play with fire?

JULIE. Not for me. I am insured.

JEAN. [*Boldly*] No, you are not. And even if you were, there are inflammable surroundings to be counted with.

JULIE. That's you, I suppose?

JEAN. Yes. Not because I am I, but because I am a young man——

JULIE. Of handsome appearance—what an incredible conceit! A Don Juan, perhaps. Or a Joseph? On my soul, I think you are a Joseph!

JEAN. Do you?

JULIE. I fear it almost.

JEAN *goes boldly up to her and takes her around the waist in order to kiss her.*

JULIE. [*Gives him a cuff on the ear*] Shame!

JEAN. Was that in play or in earnest?

JULIE. In earnest.

JEAN. Then you were in earnest a moment ago also. Your playing is too serious, and that's the dangerous thing about it. Now I am tired of playing, and I ask to be excused in order to resume my work. The count wants his boots to be ready for him, and it is after midnight already.

JULIE. Put away the boots.

JEAN. No, it's my work, which I am bound to do. But I have not undertaken to be your playmate. It's something I can never become— I hold myself too good for it.

JULIE. You're proud!

JEAN. In some ways, and not in others.

JULIE. Have you ever been in love?

JEAN. We don't use that word. But I have been fond of a lot of girls, and once I was taken sick because I couldn't have the one I wanted: sick, you know, like those princes in the Arabian Nights who cannot eat or drink for sheer love.

JULIE. Who was it?

JEAN *remains silent.*

JULIE. Who was it?

JEAN. You cannot make me tell you.

JULIE. If I ask you as an equal, ask you as—a friend: who was it?

JEAN. It was you.

JULIE. [*Sits down*] How funny!

JEAN. Yes, as you say—it was ludicrous. That was the story, you see, which I didn't want to tell you a while ago. But now I am going to tell it. Do you know how the world looks from below—no, you don't. No more than do hawks and falcons, of whom we never see the back because they are always floating about high up in the sky. I lived in the cotter's hovel, together with seven other children, and a pig—out there on the grey plain, where there isn't a single tree. But from our windows I could see the wall around the count's park, and apple-trees above it. That was the Garden of Eden, and many fierce angels were guarding it with flaming swords. Nevertheless I and some other boys found our way to the Tree of Life—now you despise me?

JULIE. Oh, stealing apples is something all boys do.

JEAN. You may say so now, but you despise me nevertheless. However—once I got into the Garden of Eden with my mother to weed the onion beds. Near by stood a Turkish pavillion, shaded by trees and covered with honeysuckle. I didn't know what it was used for, but I had never seen a more beautiful building. People went in and came out again, and one day the door was left wide open. I stole up and saw the walls covered with pictures of kings and emperors, and the windows were hung with red, fringed curtains—now you know what I mean. I— [*breaks off a lilac sprig and holds it under* MISS JULIE'S *nose*]—I had never been inside the manor, and I had never seen anything but the church—and this was much finer. No matter where my thoughts ran, they returned always—to that place. And gradually a longing arose within me to taste the full pleasure of—*enfin!* I sneaked in, looked and admired. Then I heard somebody coming. There was only one way out for fine people, but for me there was another, and I could do nothing else but choose it.

JULIE, *who has taken the lilac sprig, lets it drop on the table.*

JEAN. Then I started to run, plunged through a hedge of raspberry bushes, chased right across a strawberry plantation, and came out on the terrace where the roses grow. There I caught sight of a pink dress and pair of white stockings—that was you! I crawled under a pile of weeds—right into it, you know—into stinging thistles and wet, ill-smelling dirt. And I saw you walking among the roses, and I thought: if it be possible for a robber to get into heaven and dwell with the angels, then it is strange that a cotter's child, here on God's own earth, cannot get into the park and play with the count's daughter.

JULIE. [*Sentimentally*] Do you think all poor children have the same thoughts as you had in this case?

JEAN. [*Hesitatingly at first; then with conviction*] If *all* poor—yes—of course. Of course!

JULIE. It must be a dreadful misfortune to be poor.

JEAN. [*In a tone of deep distress and with rather exaggerated emphasis*] Oh, Miss Julie! Oh!— A dog may lie on her ladyship's sofa; a horse may have his nose patted by the young lady's hand, but a servant—[*changing his tone*]—oh well, here and there you meet one made of different stuff, and he makes a way for himself in the world, but how often does it happen?— However, do you know what I did? I jumped into the mill brook with my clothes on, and was pulled out, and got a licking. But the next Sunday, when my father and the rest of the people were going over to my grandmother's, I fixed it so that I could stay at home. And then I washed myself with soap and hot water, and put on my best clothes, and went to church, where I could see you. I did see you, and went home determined to die. But I wanted to die beautifully and pleasantly, without any pain. And then I recalled that it was dangerous to sleep under an elder bush. We had a big one that was in full bloom. I robbed it of all its flowers, and then I put them in the big box where the oats were kept and lay down in them. Did you ever notice the smoothness of oats? Soft to the touch as the skin of the human body! However, I pulled down the lid and closed my eyes—fell asleep and was waked up a very sick boy. But I didn't die, as you can see. What I wanted—that's more than I can tell. Of course, there was not the least hope of winning you—but you symbolised the hopelessness of trying to get out of the class into which I was born.

JULIE. You narrate splendidly, do you know! Did you ever go to school?

JEAN. A little. But I have read a lot of novels and gone to the theatre a good deal. And besides, I have listened to the talk of better-class people, and from that I have learned most of all.

JULIE. Do you stand around and listen to what we are saying?

JEAN. Of course! And I have heard a lot, too, when I was on the box of the carriage, or rowing the boat. Once I heard you, Miss Julie, and one of your girl friends——

JULIE. Oh!— What was it you heard then?

JEAN. Well, it wouldn't be easy to repeat. But I was rather surprised, and I couldn't understand where you had learned all those words. Perhaps, at bottom, there isn't quite so much difference as they think between one kind of people and another.

JULIE. You ought to be ashamed of yourself! We don't live as you do when we are engaged.

JEAN. [*Looking hard at her*] Is it so certain?— Well, Miss Julie, it won't pay to make yourself out so very innocent to me——

JULIE. The man on whom I bestowed my love was a scoundrel.

JEAN. That's what you always say—afterwards.

JULIE. Always?

JEAN. Always, I believe, for I have heard the same words used several times before, on similar occasions.

JULIE. What occasions?

JEAN. Like the one of which we were speaking. The last time——

JULIE. [*Rising*] Stop! I don't want to hear any more!

JEAN. Nor did *she*—curiously enough! Well, then I ask permission to go to bed.

JULIE. [*Gently*] Go to bed on Midsummer Eve?

JEAN. Yes, for dancing with that mob out there has really no attraction for me.

JULIE. Get the key to the boat and take me out on the lake— I want to watch the sunrise.

JEAN. Would that be wise?

JULIE. It sounds as if you were afraid of your reputation.

JEAN. Why not? I don't care to be made ridiculous, and I don't care to be discharged without a recommendation, for I am trying to get on in the world. And then I feel myself under a certain obligation to Christine.

JULIE. So it's Christine now——

JEAN. Yes, but it's you also— Take my advice and go to bed!

JULIE. Am I to obey you?

JEAN. For once—and for your own sake! The night is far gone. Sleepiness makes us drunk, and the head grows hot. Go to bed! And besides—if I am not mistaken—I can hear the crowd coming this way to look for me. And if we are found together here, you are lost!

CHORUS. [*Is heard approaching*]:
> Through the fields come two ladies a-walking,
> Treederee-derallah, treederee-derah.
> And one has her shoes full of water,
> Treederee-derallah-lah.
>
> They're talking of hundreds of dollars,
> Treederee-derallah, treederee-derah.
> But have not between them a dollar,
> Treederee-derallah-lah.
>
> This wreath I give you gladly,
> Treederee-derallah, treederee-derah.
> But love another madly,
> Treederee-derallah-lah.

JULIE. I know the people, and I love them, just as they love me. Let them come, and you'll see.

JEAN. No, Miss Julie, they don't love you. They take your food and spit at your back. Believe me. Listen to me—can't you hear what they are singing?— No, don't pay any attention to it!

JULIE. [*Listening*] What is it they are singing?

JEAN. Oh, something scurrilous. About you and me.

JULIE. How infamous! They ought to be ashamed! And the treachery of it!

JEAN. The mob is always cowardly. And in such a fight as this there is nothing to do but to run away.

JULIE. Run away? Where to? We cannot get out. And we cannot go into Christine's room.

JEAN. Oh, we cannot? Well, into my room, then! Necessity knows no law. And you can trust me, for I am your true and frank and respectful friend.

JULIE. But think only—think if they should look for you in there!

JEAN. I shall bolt the door. And if they try to break it open, I'll shoot!—Come! [*Kneeling before her*] Come!

JULIE. [*Meaningly*] And you promise me——?

JEAN. I swear!

> MISS JULIE *goes quickly out to the right.*
> JEAN *follows her eagerly.*

BALLET

The peasants enter. They are decked out in their best and carry flowers in their hats. A fiddler leads them. On the table they place a barrel of small-beer and a keg of "brännvin," or white Swedish whiskey, both of them decorated with wreathes woven out of leaves. First they drink. Then they form a ring and sing and dance to the melody heard before:

> "Through the fields come two ladies a-walking."

The dance finished, they leave singing.

JULIE. [*Enters alone. On seeing the disorder in the kitchen, she claps her hands together. Then she takes out a powder-puff and begins to powder her face.*

JEAN. [*Enters in a state of exaltation*] There you see! And you heard, didn't you? Do you think it possible to stay here?

JULIE. No, I don't think so. But what are we to do?

JEAN. Run away, travel, far away from here.

JULIE. Travel? Yes—but where?

JEAN. To Switzerland, the Italian lakes—you have never been there?

JULIE. No. Is the country beautiful?

JEAN. Oh! Eternal summer! Orange trees! Laurels! Oh!

JULIE. But then—what are we to do down there?

JEAN. I'll start a hotel, everything first class, including the customers.

JULIE. Hotel?

JEAN. That's the life, I tell you! Constantly new faces and new languages. Never a minute free for nerves or brooding. No trouble about what to do—for the work is calling to be done: night and day, bells that ring, trains that whistle, 'busses that come and go; and gold pieces raining on the counter all the time. That's the life for you!

JULIE. Yes, that is life. And I?

JEAN. The mistress of everything, the chief ornament of the house. With your looks—and your manners—oh, success will be assured! Enormous! You'll sit like a queen in the office and keep the slaves going by the touch of an electric button. The guests will pass in review before your throne and timidly deposit their treasures on your table. You cannot imagine how people tremble when a bill is presented to them—I'll salt the items, and you'll sugar them with your sweetest smiles. Oh, let us get away from here—[*pulling a time-table from his pocket*]—at once, with the next train! We'll be in Malmö at 6.30; in Hamburg at 8.40 to-morrow morning; in Frankfort and Basel a day later. And to reach Como by way of the St. Gotthard it will take us—let me see—three days. Three days!

JULIE. All that is all right. But you must give me some courage—Jean. Tell me that you love me. Come and take me in your arms.

JEAN. [*Reluctantly*] I should like to—but I don't dare. Not in this house again. I love you—beyond doubt—or, can you doubt it, Miss Julie?

JULIE. [*With modesty and true womanly feeling*] Miss?—Call me Julie. Between us there can be no barriers hereafter. Call me Julie!

JEAN. [*Disturbed*] I cannot! There will be barriers between us as long as we stay in this house—there is the past, and there is the count—and I have never met another person for whom I felt such respect. If I only catch sight of his gloves on a chair I feel small. If I only hear that bell up there, I jump like a shy horse. And even now, when I see his boots standing there so stiff and perky, it is as if something made my back bend. [*Kicking at the boots*] It's nothing but superstition and tradition hammered into us from childhood—but it can be as easily forgotten again. Let us only get to another country, where they have a republic, and you'll see them bend their backs double before my liveried porter. You see, backs have to be bent, but not mine. I wasn't born to that kind of thing. There's better stuff in me—character—and if I only get hold of the first branch, you'll see me do some climbing. To-day I am a valet, but next year I'll be a hotel owner. In ten years I can live on the money I have made, and then I'll go to Roumania and get myself an order. And I may—note well that I say *may*—end my days as a count.

JULIE. Splendid, splendid!

JEAN. Yes, in Roumania the title of count can be had for cash, and so you'll be a countess after all. My countess!

JULIE. What do I care about all I now cast behind me! Tell me that you love me: otherwise—yes, what am I otherwise?

JEAN. I will tell you so a thousand times—later. But not here. And above all, no sentimentality, or everything will be lost. We must look at the matter in cold blood, like sensible people. [*Takes out a cigar, cuts off the point, and lights it*] Sit down there now, and I'll sit here, and then we'll talk as if nothing had happened.

JULIE. [*In despair*] Good Lord! Have you then no feelings at all?

JEAN. I? No one is more full of feeling than I am. But I know how to control myself.

JULIE. A while ago you kissed my shoe—and now!

JEAN. [*Severely*] Yes, that was then. Now we have other things to think of.

JULIE. Don't speak harshly to me!

JEAN. No, but sensibly. One folly has been committed—don't let us commit any more! The count may be here at any moment, and before he comes our fate must be settled. What do you think of my plans for the future? Do you approve of them?

JULIE. They seem acceptable, on the whole. But there is one question: a big undertaking of that kind will require a big capital—have you got it?

JEAN. [*Chewing his cigar*] I? Of course! I have my expert knowledge, my vast experience, my familiarity with several languages. That's the very best kind of capital, I should say.

JULIE. But it won't buy you a railroad ticket even.

JEAN. That's true enough. And that is just why I am looking for a backer to advance the needful cash.

JULIE. Where could you get one all of a sudden?

JEAN. It's for you to find him if you want to become my partner.

JULIE. I cannot do it, and I have nothing myself.   [*Pause.*

JEAN. Well, then that's off——

JULIE. And——

JEAN. Everything remains as before.

JULIE. Do you think I am going to stay under this roof as your concubine? Do you think I'll let the people point their fingers at me? Do you think I can look my father in the face after this? No, take me away from here, from all this humiliation and disgrace!— Oh, what have I done? My God, my God!   [*Breaks into tears.*

JEAN. So we have got around to that tune now!— What you have done? Nothing but what many others have done before you.

JULIE. [*Crying hysterically*] And now you're despising me!—I'm falling, I'm falling!

JEAN. Fall down to me, and I'll lift you up again afterwards.

JULIE. What horrible power drew me to you? Was it the attraction which the strong exercises on the weak—the one who is rising on one who is falling? Or was it love? This—love! Do you know what love is?

JEAN. I? Well, I should say so! Don't you think I have been there before?

JULIE. Oh, the language you use, and the thoughts you think!

JEAN. Well, that's the way I was brought up, and that's the way I am. Don't get nerves now and play the exquisite, for now one of us is just as good as the other. Look here, my girl, let me treat you to a glass of something superfine.

He opens the table-drawer, takes out the wine bottle and fills up two glasses that have already been used.

JULIE. Where did you get that wine?

JEAN. In the cellar.

JULIE. My father's Burgundy!

JEAN. Well, isn't it good enough for the son-in-law?

JULIE. And I am drinking beer—I!

JEAN. It shows merely that I have better taste than you.

JULIE. Thief!

JEAN. Do you mean to tell on me?

JULIE. Oh, oh! The accomplice of a house thief! Have I been drunk, or have I been dreaming all this night? Midsummer Eve! The feast of innocent games——

JEAN. Innocent—hm!

JULIE. [*Walking back and forth*] Can there be another human being on earth so unhappy as I am at this moment?

JEAN. But why should you be? After such a conquest? Think of Christine in there. Don't you think she has feelings also?

JULIE. I thought so a while ago, but I don't think so any longer. No, a menial is a menial——

JEAN. And a whore a whore!

JULIE. [*On her knees, with folded hands*] O God in heaven, make an end of this wretched life! Take me out of the filth into which I am sinking! Save me! Save me!

JEAN. I cannot deny that I feel sorry for you. When I was lying among the onions and saw you up there among the roses—I'll tell you now—I had the same nasty thoughts that all boys have.

JULIE. And you who wanted to die for my sake!

JEAN. Among the oats. That was nothing but talk.

JULIE. Lies in other words!

JEAN. [*Beginning to feel sleepy*] Just about. I think I read the story in a paper, and it was about a chimney-sweep who crawled into a wood-box full of lilacs because a girl had brought suit against him for not support-ing her kid——

JULIE. So that's the sort you are——

JEAN. Well, I had to think of something—for it's the high-faluting stuff that the women bite on.

JULIE. Scoundrel!

JEAN. Rot!

JULIE. And now you have seen the back of the hawk——

JEAN. Well, I don't know——

JULIE. And I was to be the first branch——

JEAN. But the branch was rotten——

JULIE. I was to be the sign in front of the hotel——

JEAN. And I the hotel——

JULIE. Sit at your counter, and lure your customers, and doctor your bills——

JEAN. No, that I should have done myself——

JULIE. That a human soul can be so steeped in dirt!

JEAN. Well, wash it off!

JULIE. You lackey, you menial, stand up when I talk to you!

JEAN. You lackey-love, you mistress of a menial—shut up and get out of here! You're the right one to come and tell me that I am vulgar. People of my kind would never in their lives act as vulgarly as you have acted to-night. Do you think any servant girl would go for a man as you did? Did you ever see a girl of my class throw herself at anybody in that way? I have never seen the like of it except among beasts and prostitutes.

JULIE. [*Crushed*] That's right: strike me, step on me—I haven't de-served any better! I am a wretched creature. But help me! Help me out of this, if there be any way to do so!

JEAN. [*In a milder tone*] I don't want to lower myself by a denial of my share in the honour of seducing. But do you think a person in my place would have dared to raise his eyes to you, if the invitation to do so had not come from yourself? I am still sitting here in a state of utter surprise——

JULIE. And pride——

JEAN. Yes, why not? Although I must confess that the victory was too easy to bring with it any real intoxication.

JULIE. Strike me some more!

JEAN. [*Rising*] No! Forgive me instead what I have been saying. I don't want to strike one who is disarmed, and least of all a lady. On one hand I cannot deny that it has given me pleasure to discover that what has dazzled us below is nothing but cat-gold;[1] that the hawk is simply grey on the back also; that there is powder on the tender cheek; that there may be black borders on the polished nails; and that the handkerchief may be dirty, although it smells of perfume. But on the other hand it hurts me to have discovered that what I was striving to reach is neither better nor more genuine. It hurts me to see you sinking so low that you are far beneath your own cook—it hurts me as it hurts to see the Fall flowers beaten down by the rain and turned into mud.

JULIE. You speak as if you were already above me?

JEAN. Well, so I am. Don't you see: I could have made a countess of you, but you could never make me a count.

JULIE. But I am born of a count, and that's more than you can ever achieve.

JEAN. That's true. But I might be the father of counts—if——

JULIE. But you are a thief—and I am not.

JEAN. Thief is not the worst. There are other kinds still farther down. And then, when I serve in a house, I regard myself in a sense as a member of the family, as a child of the house, and you don't call it theft when children pick a few of the berries that load down the vines. [*His passion is aroused once more*] Miss Julie, you are a magnificent woman, and far too good for one like me. You were swept along by a spell of intoxication, and now you want to cover up your mistake by making yourself believe that you are in love with me. Well, you are not, unless possibly my looks might tempt you—in which case your love is no better than mine. I could never rest satisfied with having you care for nothing in me but the mere animal, and your love I can never win.

JULIE. Are you so sure of that?

JEAN. You mean to say that it might be possible? That I might love you: yes, without doubt—for you are beautiful, refined, [*goes up to her and takes hold of her hand*] educated, charming when you want to be so, and it is not likely that the flame will ever burn out in a man who has once been set on fire by you. [*Puts his arm around her waist*] You are like burnt wine with strong spices in it, and one of your kisses——

He tries to lead her away, but she frees herself gently from his hold.

JULIE. Leave me alone! In that way you cannot win me.

1. *cat-gold*] yellow mica.

JEAN. How then?— Not in that way! Not by caresses and sweet words! Not by thought for the future, by escape from disgrace! How then?

JULIE. How? How? I don't know— Not at all! I hate you as I hate rats, but I cannot escape from you!

JEAN. Escape *with* me!

JULIE. [*Straightening up*] Escape? Yes, we must escape!— But I am so tired. Give me a glass of wine.

JEAN *pours out wine.*

JULIE. [*Looks at her watch*] But we must have a talk first. We have still some time left.   [*Empties her glass and holds it out for more.*

JEAN. Don't drink so much. It will go to your head.

JULIE. What difference would that make?

JEAN. What difference would it make? It's vulgar to get drunk— What was it you wanted to tell me?

JULIE. We must get away. But first we must have a talk—that is, I must talk, for so far you have done all the talking. You have told me about your life. Now I must tell you about mine, so that we know each other right to the bottom before we begin the journey together.

JEAN. One moment, pardon me! Think first, so that you don't regret it afterwards, when you have already given up the secrets of your life.

JULIE. Are you not my friend?

JEAN. Yes, at times—but don't rely on me.

JULIE. You only talk like that—and besides, my secrets are known to everybody. You see, my mother was not of noble birth, but came of quite plain people. She was brought up in the ideas of her time about equality, and woman's independence, and that kind of thing. And she had a decided aversion to marriage. Therefore, when my father proposed to her, she said she wouldn't marry him—and then she did it just the same. I came into the world—against my mother's wish, I have come to think. Then my mother wanted to bring me up in a perfectly natural state, and at the same time I was to learn everything that a boy is taught, so that I might prove that a woman is just as good as a man. I was dressed as a boy, and was taught how to handle a horse, but could have nothing to do with the cows. I had to groom and harness and go hunting on horseback. I was even forced to learn something about agriculture. And all over the estate men were set to do women's work, and women to do men's—with the result that everything went to pieces and we became the laughing-stock of the whole neighbourhood. At last my father must have recovered from the spell cast over him, for he rebelled, and everything was changed to suit his own ideas. My mother was taken sick—what kind of sickness it was I don't know, but she fell often into convulsions, and she used to hide herself in the garret or in the garden, and sometimes she stayed out all night. Then came the big fire, of which you have heard. The house, the stable, and the barn were burned down, and this under circumstances which made it look as if the fire had been set on purpose. For the disaster occurred the day after our insurance expired, and the money sent for renewal of the policy had been delayed by the messenger's carelessness, so that it came too late. [*She fills her glass again and drinks.*]

JEAN. Don't drink any more.

JULIE. Oh, what does it matter!— We were without a roof over our heads and had to sleep in the carriages. My father didn't know where to get money for the rebuilding of the house. Then my mother suggested that he try to borrow from a childhood friend of hers, a brick manufacturer living not far from here. My father got the loan, but was not permitted to pay any interest, which astonished him. And so the house was built up again. [*Drinks again*] Do you know who set fire to the house?

JEAN. Her ladyship, your mother!

JULIE. Do you know who the brick manufacturer was?

JEAN. Your mother's lover?

JULIE. Do you know to whom the money belonged?

JEAN. Wait a minute—no, that I don't know.

JULIE. To my mother.

JEAN. In other words, to the count, if there was no settlement.

JULIE. There was no settlement. My mother possessed a small fortune of her own which she did not want to leave in my father's control, so she invested it with—her friend.

JEAN. Who copped it.

JULIE. Exactly! He kept it. All this came to my father's knowledge. He couldn't bring suit; he couldn't pay his wife's lover; he couldn't prove that it was his wife's money. That was my mother's revenge because he had made himself master in his own house. At that time he came near shooting himself—it was even rumoured that he had tried and failed. But he took a new lease of life, and my mother had to pay for what she had done. I can tell you that those were five years I'll never forget! My sympathies were with my father, but I took my mother's side because I was not aware of the true circumstances. From her I learned to suspect and hate men—for she hated the whole sex, as you have probably heard— and I promised her on my oath that I would never become a man's slave.

JEAN. And so you became engaged to the County Attorney.

JULIE. Yes, in order that he should be my slave.

JEAN. And he didn't want to?

JULIE. Oh, he wanted, but I wouldn't let him. I got tired of him.

JEAN. Yes, I saw it—in the stable-yard.

JULIE. What did you see?

JEAN. Just that—how he broke the engagement.

JULIE. That's a lie! It was I who broke it. Did he say he did it, the scoundrel?

JEAN. Oh, he was no scoundrel, I guess. So you hate men, Miss Julie?

JULIE. Yes! Most of the time. But now and then—when the weakness comes over me—oh, what shame!

JEAN. And you hate me too?

JULIE. Beyond measure! I should like to kill you like a wild beast——

JEAN. As you make haste to shoot a mad dog. Is that right?

JULIE. That's right!

JEAN. But now there is nothing to shoot with—and there is no dog. What are we to do then?

JULIE. Go abroad.

JEAN. In order to plague each other to death?

JULIE. No—in order to enjoy ourselves: a couple of days, a week, as long as enjoyment is possible. And then—die!

JEAN. Die? How silly! Then I think it's much better to start a hotel.

JULIE. [*Without listening to* JEAN]—At Lake Como, where the sun is always shining, and the laurels stand green at Christmas, and the oranges are glowing.

JEAN. Lake Como is a rainy hole, and I could see no oranges except in the groceries. But it is a good place for tourists, as it has a lot of villas that can be rented to loving couples, and that's a profitable business—do you know why? Because they take a lease for six months—and then they leave after three weeks.

JULIE. [*Naïvely*] Why after three weeks?

JEAN. Because they quarrel, of course. But the rent has to be paid just the same. And then you can rent the house again. And that way it goes on all the time, for there is plenty of love—even if it doesn't last long.

JULIE. You don't want to die with me?

JEAN. I don't want to die at all. Both because I am fond of living, and because I regard suicide as a crime against the Providence which has bestowed life on us.

JULIE. Do you mean to say that *you* believe in God?

JEAN. Of course, I do. And I go to church every other Sunday. Frankly speaking, now I am tired of all this, and now I am going to bed.

JULIE. So! And you think that will be enough for me? Do you know what you owe a woman that you have spoiled?

JEAN. [*Takes out his purse and throws a silver coin on the table*] You're welcome! I don't want to be in anybody's debt.

JULIE. [*Pretending not to notice the insult*] Do you know what the law provides——

JEAN. Unfortunately the law provides no punishment for a woman who seduces a man.

JULIE. [*As before*] Can you think of any escape except by our going abroad and getting married, and then getting a divorce?

JEAN. Suppose I refuse to enter into this *mésalliance?*

JULIE. *Mésalliance——*

JEAN. Yes, for me. You see, I have better ancestry than you, for nobody in my family was ever guilty of arson.

JULIE. How do you know?

JEAN. Well, nothing is known to the contrary, for we keep no pedigrees—except in the police bureau. But I have read about your pedigree in a book that was lying on the drawing-room table. Do you know who was your first ancestor? A miller who let his wife sleep with the king one night during the war with Denmark. I have no such ancestry. I have none at all, but I can become an ancestor myself.

JULIE. That's what I get for unburdening my heart to one not worthy of it; for sacrificing my family's honour——

JEAN. Dishonour! Well, what was it I told you? You shouldn't drink, for then you talk. And you *must* not talk!

JULIE. Oh, how I regret what I have done! How I regret it! If at least you loved me!

JEAN. For the last time: what do you mean? Am I to weep? Am I to jump over your whip? Am I to kiss you, and lure you down to Lake Como for three weeks, and so on? What am I to do? What do you expect? This is getting to be rather painful! But that's what comes from getting mixed up with women. Miss Julie! I see that you are unhappy; I know that you are suffering; but I cannot understand you. We never carry on like that. There is never any hatred between us. Love is to us a play, and we play at it when our work leaves us time to do so. But we have not the time to do so all day and all night, as you have. I believe you are sick—I am sure you are sick.

JULIE. You should be good to me—and now you speak like a human being.

JEAN. All right, but be human yourself. You spit on me, and then you won't let me wipe myself—on you!

JULIE. Help me, help me! Tell me only what I am to do—where I am to turn?

JEAN. O Lord, if I only knew that myself!

JULIE. I have been exasperated, I have been mad, but there ought to be some way of saving myself.

JEAN. Stay right here and keep quiet. Nobody knows anything.

JULIE. Impossible! The people know, and Christine knows.

JEAN. They don't know, and they would never believe it possible.—

JULIE. [Hesitating] But—it might happen again.

JEAN. That's true.

JULIE. And the results?

JEAN. [Frightened] The results! Where was my head when I didn't think of that! Well, then there is only one thing to do—you must leave. At once! I can't go with you, for then everything would be lost, so you must go alone—abroad—anywhere!

JULIE. Alone? Where?— I can't do it.

JEAN. You must! And before the count gets back. If you stay, then you know what will happen. Once on the wrong path, one wants to keep on, as the harm is done anyhow. Then one grows more and more reckless—and at last it all comes out. So you must get away! Then you can write to the count and tell him everything, except that it was me. And he would never guess it. Nor do I think he would be very anxious to find out.

JULIE. I'll go if you come with me.

JEAN. Are you stark mad, woman? Miss Julie to run away with her valet! It would be in the papers in another day, and the count could never survive it.

JULIE. I can't leave! I can't stay! Help me! I am so tired, so fearfully tired. Give me orders! Set me going, for I can no longer think, no longer act——

JEAN. Do you see now what good-for-nothings you are! Why do you strut and turn up your noses as if you were the lords of creation? Well, I am going to give you orders. Go up and dress. Get some travelling money, and then come back again.

JULIE. [In an undertone] Come up with me!

JEAN. To your room? Now you're crazy again! [Hesitates a moment] No, you must go at once! [Takes her by the hand and leads her out.

JULIE. [On her way out] Can't you speak kindly to me, Jean?

JEAN. An order must always sound unkind. Now you can find out how it feels!

JULIE *goes out.*

JEAN, *alone, draws a sigh of relief; sits down at the table; takes out a note-book and a pencil; figures aloud from time to time; dumb play until* CHRISTINE *enters dressed for church; she has a false shirt front and a white tie in one of her hands.*

CHRISTINE. Goodness gracious, how the place looks! What have you been up to anyhow?

JEAN. Oh, it was Miss Julie who dragged in the people. Have you been sleeping so hard that you didn't hear anything at all?

CHRISTINE. I have been sleeping like a log.

JEAN. And dressed for church already?

CHRISTINE. Yes, didn't you promise to come with me to communion to-day?

JEAN. Oh, yes, I remember now. And there you've got the finery. Well, come on with it.   [*Sits down;* CHRISTINE *helps him to put on the shirt front and the white tie.*

[*Pause.*

JEAN. [*Sleepily*] What's the text to-day?

CHRISTINE. Oh, about John the Baptist beheaded, I guess.

JEAN. That's going to be a long story, I'm sure. My, but you choke me! Oh, I'm so sleepy, so sleepy!

CHRISTINE. Well, what has been keeping you up all night? Why, man, you're just green in the face!

JEAN. I have been sitting here talking with Miss Julie.

CHRISTINE. She hasn't an idea of what's proper, that creature! [*Pause.*

JEAN. Say, Christine.

CHRISTINE. Well?

JEAN. Isn't it funny anyhow, when you come to think of it? Her!

CHRISTINE. What is it that's funny?

JEAN. Everything!   [*Pause.*

CHRISTINE. [*Seeing the glasses on the table that are only half emptied*] So you've been drinking together also?

JEAN. Yes.

CHRISTINE. Shame on you! Look me in the eye!

JEAN. Yes.

CHRISTINE. Is it possible? Is it possible?

JEAN. [*After a moment's thought*] Yes, it is!

CHRISTINE. Ugh! That's worse than I could ever have believed. It's awful!

JEAN. You are not jealous of her, are you?

CHRISTINE. No, not of her. Had it been Clara or Sophie, then I'd have scratched your eyes out. Yes, that's the way I feel about it, and I can't tell why. Oh my, but that was nasty!

JEAN. Are you mad at her then?

CHRISTINE. No, but at you! It was wrong of you, very wrong! Poor girl! No, I tell you, I don't want to stay in this house any longer, with people for whom it is impossible to have any respect.

JEAN. Why should you have any respect for them?

CHRISTINE. And you who are such a smarty can't tell that! You wouldn't serve people who don't act decently, would you? It's to lower oneself, I think.

JEAN. Yes, but it ought to be a consolation to us that they are not a bit better than we.

CHRISTINE. No, I don't think so. For if they're no better, then it's no use trying to get up to them. And just think of the count! Think of him who has had so much sorrow in his day! No, I don't want to stay any longer in this house— And with a fellow like you, too. If it had been the County Attorney—if it had only been some one of her own sort——

JEAN. Now look here!

CHRISTINE. Yes, yes! You're all right in your way, but there's after all some difference between one kind of people and another— No, but this is something I'll never get over!— And the young lady who was so proud, and so tart to the men, that you couldn't believe she would ever let one come near her—and such a one at that! And she who wanted to have poor Diana shot because she had been running around with the gate-keeper's pug!— Well, I declare!— But I won't stay here any longer, and next October I get out of here.

JEAN. And then?

CHRISTINE. Well, as we've come to talk of that now, perhaps it would be just as well if you looked for something, seeing that we're going to get married after all.

JEAN. Well, what could I look for? As a married man I couldn't get a place like this.

CHRISTINE. No, I understand that. But you could get a job as a janitor, or maybe as a messenger in some government bureau. Of course, the public loaf is always short in weight, but it comes steady, and then there is a pension for the widow and the children——

JEAN. [Making a face] That's good and well, but it isn't my style to think of dying all at once for the sake of wife and children. I must say that my plans have been looking toward something better than that kind of thing.

CHRISTINE. Your plans, yes—but you've got obligations also, and those you had better keep in mind!

JEAN. Now don't you get my dander up by talking of obligations! I know what I've got to do anyhow. [*Listening for some sound on the outside*] However, we've plenty of time to think of all this. Go in now and get ready, and then we'll go to church.

CHRISTINE. Who is walking around up there?

JEAN. I don't know, unless it be Clara.

CHRISTINE. [*Going out*] It can't be the count, do you think, who's come home without anybody hearing him?

JEAN. [*Scared*] The count? No, that isn't possible, for then he would have rung for me.

CHRISTINE. [*As she goes out*] Well, God help us all! Never have I seen the like of it!

> The sun has risen and is shining on the tree tops in the park. The light changes gradually until it comes slantingly in through the windows. JEAN *goes to the door and gives a signal.*

JULIE. [*Enters in travelling dress and carrying a small bird-cage covered up with a towel; this she places on a chair*] Now I am ready.

JEAN. Hush! Christine is awake.

JULIE. [*Showing extreme nervousness during the following scene*] Did she suspect anything?

JEAN. She knows nothing at all. But, my heavens, how you look!

JULIE. How do I look?

JEAN. You're as pale as a corpse, and—pardon me, but your face is dirty.

JULIE. Let me wash it then— Now! [*She goes over to the washstand and washes her face and hands*] Give me a towel— Oh!— That's the sun rising!

JEAN. And then the ogre bursts.

JULIE. Yes, ogres and trolls were abroad last night!— But listen, Jean. Come with me, for now I have the money.

JEAN. [*Doubtfully*] Enough?

JULIE. Enough to start with. Come with me, for I cannot travel alone to-day. Think of it—Midsummer Day, on a stuffy train, jammed with people who stare at you—and standing still at stations when you want to fly. No, I cannot! I cannot! And then the memories will come: childhood memories of Midsummer Days, when the inside of the church was turned into a green forest—birches and lilacs; the dinner at the festive table with relatives and friends; the afternoon in the park, with dancing and music, flowers and games! Oh, you may run and run, but your memories are in the baggage-car, and with them remorse and repentance!

JEAN. I'll go with you—but at once, before it's too late. This very moment!

JULIE. Well, get dressed then.   [Picks up the cage.

JEAN. But no baggage! That would only give us away.

JULIE. No, nothing at all! Only what we can take with us in the car.

JEAN. [Has taken down his hat] What have you got there? What is it?

JULIE. It's only my finch. I can't leave it behind.

JEAN. Did you ever! Dragging a bird-cage along with us! You must be raving mad! Drop the cage!

JULIE. The only thing I take with me from my home! The only living creature that loves me since Diana deserted me! Don't be cruel! Let me take it along!

JEAN. Drop the cage, I tell you! And don't talk so loud—Christine can hear us.

JULIE. No, I won't let it fall into strange hands. I'd rather have you kill it!

JEAN. Well, give it to me, and I'll wring its neck.

JULIE. Yes, but don't hurt it. Don't—no, I cannot!

JEAN. Let me—I can!

JULIE. [Takes the bird out of the cage and kisses it] Oh, my little birdie, must it die and go away from its mistress!

JEAN. Don't make a scene, please. Don't you know it's a question of your life, of your future? Come, quick!

Snatches the bird away from her, carries it to the chopping-block and picks up an axe. MISS JULIE *turns away.*

JEAN. You should have learned how to kill chickens instead of shooting with a revolver—[brings down the axe]—then you wouldn't have fainted for a drop of blood.

JULIE. [Screaming] Kill me too! Kill me! You who can take the life of an innocent creature without turning a hair! Oh, I hate and despise you! There is blood between us! Cursed be the hour when I first met you! Cursed be the hour when I came to life in my mother's womb!

JEAN. Well, what's the use of all that cursing? Come on!

JULIE. [Approaching the chopping-block as if drawn to it against her will] No, I don't want to go yet. I cannot—I must see—Hush! There's a carriage coming up the road. [Listening without taking her eyes off the *block and the axe*] You think I cannot stand the sight of blood. You think I am as weak as that—oh, I should like to see your blood, your brains, on that block there. I should like to see your whole sex swimming in blood like that thing there. I think I could drink out of your skull, and bathe my feet in your open breast, and eat your heart from the spit!— You think I am weak; you think I love you because the fruit of my womb was yearning for your seed; you think I want to carry your offspring under my heart and nourish it with my blood—bear your children and take your name! Tell me, you, what are you called anyhow? I have never heard your family name—and maybe you haven't any. I should become Mrs. "Hovel," or Mrs. "Backyard"—you dog there, that's wearing my collar; you lackey with my coat of arms on your buttons—and I should share with my cook, and be the rival of my own servant. Oh! Oh! Oh!— You think I am a coward and want to run away! No, now I'll stay—and let the lightning strike! My father will come home—will find his chiffonier opened—the money gone! Then he'll ring—twice for the valet—and then he'll send for the sheriff—and then I shall tell everything! Everything! Oh, but it will be good to get an end to it—if it only be the end! And then his heart will break, and he dies!— So there will be an end to all of us—and all will be quiet—peace—eternal rest!— And then the coat of arms will be shattered on the coffin—and the count's line will be wiped out—but the lackey's line goes on in the orphan asylum—wins laurels in the gutter, and ends in jail.

JEAN. There spoke the royal blood! Bravo, Miss Julie! Now you put the miller back in his sack!

CHRISTINE *enters dressed for church and carrying a hymn-book in her hand.*

JULIE. [*Hurries up to her and throws herself into her arms as if seeking protection*] Help me, Christine! Help me against this man!

CHRISTINE. [*Unmoved and cold*] What kind of performance is this on the Sabbath morning? [*Catches sight of the chopping-block*] My, what a mess you have made!— What's the meaning of all this? And the way you shout and carry on!

JULIE. You are a woman, Christine, and you are my friend. Beware of that scoundrel!

JEAN. [*A little shy and embarrassed*] While the ladies are discussing I'll get myself a shave.   [*Slinks out to the right.*

JULIE. You must understand me, and you must listen to me.

CHRISTINE. No, really, I don't understand this kind of trolloping.

Where are you going in your travelling-dress—and he with his hat on—what?— What?

JULIE. Listen, Christine, listen, and I'll tell you everything——

CHRISTINE. I don't want to know anything——

JULIE. You must listen to me——

CHRISTINE. What is it about? Is it about this nonsense with Jean? Well, I don't care about it at all, for it's none of my business. But if you're planning to get him away with you, we'll put a stop to that!

JULIE. [*Extremely nervous*] Please try to be quiet, Christine, and listen to me. I cannot stay here, and Jean cannot stay here—and so we must leave——

CHRISTINE. Hm, hm!

JULIE. [*Brightening up*] But now I have got an idea, you know. Suppose all three of us should leave—go abroad—go to Switzerland and start a hotel together—I have money, you know—and Jean and I could run the whole thing—and you, I thought, could take charge of the kitchen—Wouldn't that be fine!— Say yes, now! And come along with us! Then everything is fixed!— Oh, say yes!

[*She puts her arms around* CHRISTINE *and pats her.*

CHRISTINE. [*Coldly and thoughtfully*] Hm, hm!

JULIE. [*Presto tempo*] You have never travelled, Christine—you must get out and have a look at the world. You cannot imagine what fun it is to travel on a train—constantly new people—new countries—and then we get to Hamburg and take in the Zoological Gardens in passing—that's what you like—and then we go to the theatres and to the opera—and when we get to Munich, there, you know, we have a lot of museums, where they keep Rubens and Raphael and all those big painters, you know— Haven't you heard of Munich, where King Louis used to live—the king, you know, that went mad— And then we'll have a look at his castle—he has still some castles that are furnished just as in a fairy tale—and from there it isn't very far to Switzerland—and the Alps, you know—just think of the Alps, with snow on top of them in the middle of the summer—and there you have orange trees and laurels that are green all the year around——

JEAN *is seen in the right wing, sharpening his razor on a strop which he holds between his teeth and his left hand; he listens to the talk with a pleased mien and nods approval now and then.*

JULIE. [*Tempo prestissimo*] And then we get a hotel—and I sit in the office, while Jean is outside receiving tourists—and goes out marketing—and writes letters— That's a life for you— Then the train whistles, and the 'bus drives up, and it rings upstairs, and it rings in the restaurant—and then I make out the bills—and I am going to salt them, too— You can never imagine how timid tourists are when they come to pay their bills! And you—you will sit like a queen in the kitchen. Of course, you are not going to stand at the stove yourself. And you'll have to dress neatly and nicely in order to show yourself to people—and with your looks—yes, I am not flattering you—you'll catch a husband some fine day—some rich Englishman, you know—for those fellows are so easy [*slowing down*] to catch—and then we grow rich—and we build us a villa at Lake Como—of course, it is raining a little in that place now and then—but [*limply*] the sun must be shining sometimes—although it looks dark—and—then—or else we can go home again—and come back—here—or some other place——

CHRISTINE. Tell me, Miss Julie, do you believe in all that yourself?

JULIE. [*Crushed*] Do I believe in it myself?

CHRISTINE. Yes.

JULIE. [*Exhausted*] I don't know: I believe no longer in anything. [*She sinks down on the bench and drops her head between her arms on the table*] Nothing! Nothing at all!

CHRISTINE. [*Turns to the right, where* JEAN *is standing*] So you were going to run away!

JEAN. [*Abashed, puts the razor on the table*] Run away? Well, that's putting it rather strong. You have heard what the young lady proposes, and though she is tired out now by being up all night, it's a proposition that can be put through all right.

CHRISTINE. Now you tell me: did you mean me to act as cook for that one there——?

JEAN. [*Sharply*] Will you please use decent language in speaking to your mistress! Do you understand?

CHRISTINE. Mistress!

JEAN. Yes!

CHRISTINE. Well, well! Listen to him!

JEAN. Yes, it would be better for you to listen a little more and talk a little less. Miss Julie is your mistress, and what makes you disrespectful to her now should make you feel the same way about yourself.

CHRISTINE. Oh, I have always had enough respect for myself——

JEAN. To have none for others!

CHRISTINE. —not to go below my own station. You can't say that the count's cook has had anything to do with the groom or the swineherd. You can't say anything of the kind!

JEAN. Yes, it's your luck that you have had to do with a gentleman.

CHRISTINE. Yes, a gentleman who sells the oats out of the count's stable!

JEAN. What's that to you who get a commission on the groceries and bribes from the butcher?

CHRISTINE. What's that?

JEAN. And so you can't respect your master and mistress any longer! You—you!

CHRISTINE. Are you coming with me to church? I think you need a good sermon on top of such a deed.

JEAN. No, I am not going to church to-day. You can go by yourself and confess your own deeds.

CHRISTINE. Yes, I'll do that, and I'll bring back enough forgiveness to cover you also. The Saviour suffered and died on the cross for all our sins, and if we go to him with a believing heart and a repentant mind, he'll take all our guilt on himself.

JULIE. Do you believe that, Christine?

CHRISTINE. It is my living belief, as sure as I stand here, and the faith of my childhood which I have kept since I was young, Miss Julie. And where sin abounds, grace abounds too.

JULIE. Oh, if I had your faith! Oh, if——

CHRISTINE. Yes, but you don't get it without the special grace of God, and that is not bestowed on everybody——

JULIE. On whom is it bestowed then?

CHRISTINE. That's just the great secret of the work of grace, Miss Julie, and the Lord has no regard for persons, but there those that are last shall be the foremost——

JULIE. Yes, but that means he has regard for those that are last.

CHRISTINE. [*Going right on*] —and it is easier for a camel to go through a needle's eye than for a rich man to get into heaven. That's the way it is, Miss Julie. Now I am going, however—alone—and as I pass by, I'll tell the stableman not to let out the horses if anybody should like to get away before the count comes home. Good-bye!   [*Goes out.*

JEAN. Well, ain't she a devil!— And all this for the sake of a finch!

JULIE. [*Apathetically*] Never mind the finch!— Can you see any way out of this, any way to end it?

JEAN. [*Ponders*] No!

JULIE. What would you do in my place?

JEAN. In your place? Let me see. As one of gentle birth, as a woman, as one who has—fallen. I don't know—yes, I do know!

JULIE. [*Picking up the razor with a significant gesture*] Like this?

JEAN. Yes!— But please observe that I myself wouldn't do it, for there is a difference between us.

JULIE. Because you are a man and I a woman? What is the difference?

JEAN. It is the same—as—that between man and woman.

JULIE. [*With the razor in her hand*] I want to, but I cannot!— My father couldn't either, that time he should have done it.

JEAN. No, he should not have done it, for he had to get his revenge first.

JULIE. And now it is my mother's turn to revenge herself again, through me.

JEAN. Have you not loved your father, Miss Julie?

JULIE. Yes, immensely, but I must have hated him, too. I think I must have been doing so without being aware of it. But he was the one who reared me in contempt for my own sex—half woman and half man! Whose fault is it, this that has happened? My father's—my mother's— my own? My own? Why, I have nothing that is my own. I haven't a thought that didn't come from my father; not a passion that didn't come from my mother; and now this last—this about all human creatures being equal—I got that from him, my fiancé—whom I call a scoundrel for that reason! How can it be my own fault? To put the blame on Jesus, as Christine does—no, I am too proud for that, and know too much— thanks to my father's teachings— And that about a rich person not getting into heaven, it's just a lie, and Christine, who has money in the savings-bank, wouldn't get in anyhow. Whose is the fault?— What does it matter whose it is? For just the same I am the one who must bear the guilt and the results——

JEAN. Yes, but——

> *Two sharp strokes are rung on the bell.* MISS JULIE *leaps to her feet.* JEAN *changes his coat.*

JEAN. The count is back. Think if Christine——
> [*Goes to the speaking-tube, knocks on it, and listens.*

JULIE. Now he has been to the chiffonier!

JEAN. It is Jean, your lordship! [*Listening again, the spectators being unable to hear what the count says*] Yes, your lordship! [*Listening*] Yes, your lordship! At once! [*Listening*] In a minute, your lordship! [*Listening*] Yes, yes! In half an hour!

JULIE. [*With intense concern*] What did he say? Lord Jesus, what did he say?

JEAN. He called for his boots and wanted his coffee in half an hour.

JULIE. In half an hour then! Oh, I am so tired. I can't do anything; can't repent, can't run away, can't stay, can't live—can't die! Help me now! Command me, and I'll obey you like a dog! Do me this last favour—save my honour, and save his name! You know what my will ought to do, and what it cannot do—now give me your will, and make me do it!

JEAN. I don't know why—but now I can't either—I don't understand— It is just as if this coat here made a—I cannot command you—and now, since I've heard the count's voice—now—I can't quite explain it—but— Oh, that damned menial is back in my spine again. I believe if the count should come down here, and if he should tell me to cut my own throat—I'd do it on the spot!

JULIE. Make believe that you are he, and that I am you!— You did some fine acting when you were on your knees before me—then you were the nobleman—or—have you ever been to a show and seen one who could hypnotize people?

JEAN *makes a sign of assent.*

JULIE. He says to his subject: get the broom. And the man gets it. He says: sweep. And the man sweeps.

JEAN. But then the other person must be asleep.

JULIE. [*Ecstatically*] I am asleep already—there is nothing in the whole room but a lot of smoke—and you look like a stove—that looks like a man in black clothes and a high hat—and your eyes glow like coals when the fire is going out—and your face is a lump of white ashes. [*The sunlight has reached the floor and is now falling on* JEAN] How warm and nice it is! [*She rubs her hands as if warming them before a fire*] And so light—and so peaceful!

JEAN. [*Takes the razor and puts it in her hand*] There's the broom! Go now, while it is light—to the barn—and——

[*Whispers something in her ear.*

JULIE. [*Awake*] Thank you! Now I shall have rest! But tell me first—that the foremost also receive the gift of grace. Say it, even if you don't believe it.

JEAN. The foremost? No, I can't do that!— But wait—Miss Julie—I know! You are no longer among the foremost—now when you are among the—last!

JULIE. That's right. I am among the last of all: I am the very last. Oh!— But now I cannot go— Tell me once more that I must go!

JEAN. No, now I can't do it either. I cannot!

JULIE. And those that are foremost shall be the last.

JEAN. Don't think, don't think! Why, you are taking away my strength, too, so that I become a coward— What? I thought I saw the bell moving!— To be that scared of a bell! Yes, but it isn't only the bell— there is somebody behind it—a hand that makes it move—and something else that makes the hand move—but if you cover up your ears— just cover up your ears! Then it rings worse than ever! Rings and rings, until you answer it—and then it's too late—then comes the sheriff—and then—

Two quick rings from the bell.

JEAN. [*Shrinks together; then he straightens himself up*] It's horrid! But there's no other end to it!— Go!

JULIE *goes firmly out through the door.*

Curtain.

DOVER·THRIFT·EDITIONS

NONFICTION

NARRATIVE OF THE LIFE OF FREDERICK DOUGLASS, Frederick Douglass. 96pp. 0-486-28499-9

SELF-RELIANCE AND OTHER ESSAYS, Ralph Waldo Emerson. 128pp. 0-486-27790-9

THE LIFE OF OLAUDAH EQUIANO, OR GUSTAVUS VASSA, THE AFRICAN, Olaudah Equiano. 192pp. 0-486-40661-X

THE AUTOBIOGRAPHY OF BENJAMIN FRANKLIN, Benjamin Franklin. 144pp. 0-486-29073-5

TOTEM AND TABOO, Sigmund Freud. 176pp. (Not available in Europe or United Kingdom.) 0-486-40434-X

LOVE: A Book of Quotations, Herb Galewitz (ed.). 64pp. 0-486-40004-2

PRAGMATISM, William James. 128pp. 0-486-28270-8

THE STORY OF MY LIFE, Helen Keller. 80pp. 0-486-29249-5

TAO TE CHING, Lao Tze. 112pp. 0-486-29792-6

GREAT SPEECHES, Abraham Lincoln. 112pp. 0-486-26872-1

THE PRINCE, Niccolò Machiavelli. 80pp. 0-486-27274-5

THE SUBJECTION OF WOMEN, John Stuart Mill. 112pp. 0-486-29601-6

SELECTED ESSAYS, Michel de Montaigne. 96pp. 0-486-29109-X

UTOPIA, Sir Thomas More. 96pp. 0-486-29583-4

BEYOND GOOD AND EVIL: Prelude to a Philosophy of the Future, Friedrich Nietzsche. 176pp. 0-486-29868-X

THE BIRTH OF TRAGEDY, Friedrich Nietzsche. 96pp. 0-486-28515-4

COMMON SENSE, Thomas Paine. 64pp. 0-486-29602-4

SYMPOSIUM AND PHAEDRUS, Plato. 96pp. 0-486-27798-4

THE TRIAL AND DEATH OF SOCRATES: Four Dialogues, Plato. 128pp. 0-486-27066-1

A MODEST PROPOSAL AND OTHER SATIRICAL WORKS, Jonathan Swift. 64pp. 0-486-28759-9

CIVIL DISOBEDIENCE AND OTHER ESSAYS, Henry David Thoreau. 96pp. 0-486-27563-9

WALDEN; OR, LIFE IN THE WOODS, Henry David Thoreau. 224pp. 0-486-28495-6

NARRATIVE OF SOJOURNER TRUTH, Sojourner Truth. 80pp. 0-486-29899-X

THE THEORY OF THE LEISURE CLASS, Thorstein Veblen. 256pp. 0-486-28062-4

DE PROFUNDIS, Oscar Wilde. 64pp. 0-486-29308-4

OSCAR WILDE'S WIT AND WISDOM: A Book of Quotations, Oscar Wilde. 64pp. 0-486-40146-4

UP FROM SLAVERY, Booker T. Washington. 160pp. 0-486-28738-6

A VINDICATION OF THE RIGHTS OF WOMAN, Mary Wollstonecraft. 224pp. 0-486-29036-0

PLAYS

PROMETHEUS BOUND, Aeschylus. 64pp. 0-486-28762-9

THE ORESTEIA TRILOGY: Agamemnon, The Libation-Bearers and The Furies, Aeschylus. 160pp. 0-486-29242-8

LYSISTRATA, Aristophanes. 64pp. 0-486-28225-2

WHAT EVERY WOMAN KNOWS, James Barrie. 80pp. (Not available in Europe or United Kingdom.) 0-486-29578-8

THE CHERRY ORCHARD, Anton Chekhov. 64pp. 0-486-26682-6

THE SEA GULL, Anton Chekhov. 64pp. 0-486-40656-3

THE THREE SISTERS, Anton Chekhov. 64pp. 0-486-27544-2

UNCLE VANYA, Anton Chekhov. 64pp. 0-486-40159-6

THE WAY OF THE WORLD, William Congreve. 80pp. 0-486-27787-9

BACCHAE, Euripides. 64pp. 0-486-29580-X

MEDEA, Euripides. 64pp. 0-486-27548-5

DOVER·THRIFT·EDITIONS

PLAYS

LIFE IS A DREAM, Pedro Calderón de la Barca. 96pp. 0-486-42124-4
H. M. S. PINAFORE, William Schwenck Gilbert. 64pp. 0-486-41114-1
THE MIKADO, William Schwenck Gilbert. 64pp. 0-486-27268-0
SHE STOOPS TO CONQUER, Oliver Goldsmith. 80pp. 0-486-26867-5
THE LOWER DEPTHS, Maxim Gorky. 80pp. 0-486-41115-X
A DOLL'S HOUSE, Henrik Ibsen. 80pp. 0-486-27062-9
GHOSTS, Henrik Ibsen. 64pp. 0-486-29852-3
HEDDA GABLER, Henrik Ibsen. 80pp. 0-486-26469-6
PEER GYNT, Henrik Ibsen. 144pp. 0-486-42686-6
THE WILD DUCK, Henrik Ibsen. 96pp. 0-486-41116-8
VOLPONE, Ben Jonson. 112pp. 0-486-28049-7
DR. FAUSTUS, Christopher Marlowe. 64pp. 0-486-28208-2
TAMBURLAINE, Christopher Marlowe. 128pp. 0-486-42125-2
THE IMAGINARY INVALID, Molière. 96pp. 0-486-43789-2
THE MISANTHROPE, Molière. 64pp. 0-486-27065-3
RIGHT YOU ARE, IF YOU THINK YOU ARE, Luigi Pirandello. 64pp. (Not available in Europe
    or United Kingdom.) 0-486-29576-1
SIX CHARACTERS IN SEARCH OF AN AUTHOR, Luigi Pirandello. 64pp. (Not available in
    Europe or United Kingdom.) 0-486-29992-9
PHÈDRE, Jean Racine. 64pp. 0-486-41927-4
HANDS AROUND, Arthur Schnitzler. 64pp. 0-486-28724-6
ANTONY AND CLEOPATRA, William Shakespeare. 128pp. 0-486-40062-X
AS YOU LIKE IT, William Shakespeare. 80pp. 0-486-40432-3
HAMLET, William Shakespeare. 128pp. 0-486-27278-8
HENRY IV, William Shakespeare. 96pp. 0-486-29584-2
JULIUS CAESAR, William Shakespeare. 80pp. 0-486-26876-4
KING LEAR, William Shakespeare. 112pp. 0-486-28058-6
LOVE'S LABOUR'S LOST, William Shakespeare. 64pp. 0-486-41929-0
MACBETH, William Shakespeare. 96pp. 0-486-27802-6
MEASURE FOR MEASURE, William Shakespeare. 96pp. 0-486-40889-2
THE MERCHANT OF VENICE, William Shakespeare. 96pp. 0-486-28492-1
A MIDSUMMER NIGHT'S DREAM, William Shakespeare. 80pp. 0-486-27067-X
MUCH ADO ABOUT NOTHING, William Shakespeare. 80pp. 0-486-28272-4
OTHELLO, William Shakespeare. 112pp. 0-486-29097-2
RICHARD III, William Shakespeare. 112pp. 0-486-28747-5
ROMEO AND JULIET, William Shakespeare. 96pp. 0-486-27557-4
THE TAMING OF THE SHREW, William Shakespeare. 96pp. 0-486-29765-9
THE TEMPEST, William Shakespeare. 96pp. 0-486-40658-X
TWELFTH NIGHT; OR, WHAT YOU WILL, William Shakespeare. 80pp. 0-486-29290-8
ARMS AND THE MAN, George Bernard Shaw. 80pp. (Not available in Europe or United
    Kingdom.) 0-486-26476-9
HEARTBREAK HOUSE, George Bernard Shaw. 128pp. (Not available in Europe or United
    Kingdom.) 0-486-29291-6
PYGMALION, George Bernard Shaw. 96pp. (Available in U.S. only.) 0-486-28222-8
THE RIVALS, Richard Brinsley Sheridan. 96pp. 0-486-40433-1
THE SCHOOL FOR SCANDAL, Richard Brinsley Sheridan. 96pp. 0-486-26687-7
ANTIGONE, Sophocles. 64pp. 0-486-27804-2
OEDIPUS AT COLONUS, Sophocles. 64pp. 0-486-40659-8
OEDIPUS REX, Sophocles. 64pp. 0-486-26877-2

DOVER · THRIFT · EDITIONS

PLAYS

ELECTRA, Sophocles. 64pp. 0-486-28482-4

MISS JULIE, August Strindberg. 64pp. 0-486-27281-8

THE PLAYBOY OF THE WESTERN WORLD AND RIDERS TO THE SEA, J. M. Synge. 80pp. 0-486-27562-0

THE DUCHESS OF MALFI, John Webster. 96pp. 0-486-40660-1

THE IMPORTANCE OF BEING EARNEST, Oscar Wilde. 64pp. 0-486-26478-5

LADY WINDERMERE'S FAN, Oscar Wilde. 64pp. 0-486-40078-6

BOXED SETS

FAVORITE JANE AUSTEN NOVELS: *Pride and Prejudice, Sense and Sensibility* and *Persuasion* (Complete and Unabridged), Jane Austen. 800pp. 0-486-29748-9

BEST WORKS OF MARK TWAIN: Four Books, Dover. 624pp. 0-486-40226-6

EIGHT GREAT GREEK TRAGEDIES: Six Books, Dover. 480pp. 0-486-40203-7

FIVE GREAT ENGLISH ROMANTIC POETS, Dover. 496pp. 0-486-27893-X

GREAT AFRICAN-AMERICAN WRITERS: Seven Books, Dover. 704pp. 0-486-29995-3

GREAT WOMEN POETS: 4 Complete Books, Dover. 256pp. (Available in U.S. only.) 0-486-28388-7

MASTERPIECES OF RUSSIAN LITERATURE: Seven Books, Dover. 880pp. 0-486-40665-2

SIX GREAT AMERICAN POETS: Poems by Poe, Dickinson, Whitman, Longfellow, Frost, and Millay, Dover. 512pp. (Available in U.S. only.) 0-486-27425-X

FAVORITE NOVELS AND STORIES: Four Complete Books, Jack London. 568pp. 0-486-42216-X

FIVE GREAT SCIENCE FICTION NOVELS, H. G. Wells. 640pp. 0-486-43978-X

FIVE GREAT PLAYS OF SHAKESPEARE, Dover. 496pp. 0-486-27892-1

TWELVE PLAYS BY SHAKESPEARE, William Shakespeare. 1,173pp. 0-486-44336-1